Stories on the Move

Stories on the Move

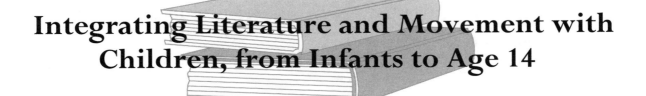

Integrating Literature and Movement with Children, from Infants to Age 14

Arlene Cohen

Illustrations by Andrea Fitcha McAllister

LIBRARIES
U N L I M I T E D
A Member of the Greenwood Publishing Group

Westport, Connecticut • London

Library of Congress Cataloging-in-Publication Data

Cohen, Arlene.
Stories on the move : integrating literature and movement with children,
   from infants to age 14 / Arlene Cohen ; illustrations by Andrea Fitcha McAllister.
      p. cm.
   Includes bibliographical references and index.
   ISBN-13: 978–1–59158–418–6 (alk. paper)
   ISBN-10: 1–59158–418–3 (alk. paper)
   1. Storytelling. 2. Activity programs in education. 3. Movement education. I. Title.
LB1042.C468 2007
372.67'7—dc22   2006102802

British Library Cataloguing in Publication Data is available.

Library of Congress Catalog Card Number: 2006102802
ISBN-13: 978–1–59158–418–6

First published in 2007

Libraries Unlimited, 88 Post Road West, Westport, CT 06881
A Member of the Greenwood Publishing Group, Inc.
www.lu.com

Printed in the United States of America

The paper used in this book complies with the
Permanent Paper Standard issued by the National
Information Standards Organization (Z39.48–1984).

10 9 8 7 6 5 4 3 2 1

To my loving grandchildren, Sydney, Sarah, and Sammy, and my daughter and son-in-law, Suzette and Shawn. I hold you in the Light.

In Gratitude to my Mentors:
Betty Jones, my dance teacher, who taught me how to "fall up" and to all the dance teachers who have shared with me the gift of dance.
To Lucille Breneman and Nyla Ching Fujii, my model Storytellers.

To my Mother
Who Sang and Danced me through Life.

To the Arts Organizations: National Foundation for Culture and the Arts, the Hawaii State Foundation on Culture and the Arts, the Hawaii Zoological Society, the Regional Arts and Culture Council in Portland, Oregon, and the schools, libraries, community centers, bookstores, and organizations who have hosted my programs during the last 30 years.

Contents

Illustrations

Tables

Figures

Drawings (Unnumbered)

Preface

What good is a story
if it sits in a book,
How much better to
invite it out for a look!

A story gets tired
lying down on a page;
stuck on a shelf,
it yellows with age.

Give a story
Some fresh air and a bright sunny day,
and it will stand up and feel very gay.
Given a chance,
it might even get up and dance.

Photo by Francis Haar

—Introduction to Moving Stories Program, written and first performed
by Arlene Cohen in 1984 for a Hawaii Artist-in-the-Schools Tour

Acknowledgments

I would like to thank my editor Barbara Ittner, Sue Stewart, and the Libraries Unlimited staff for working with me throughout the process of creating this guide.

I would like to acknowledge Multnomah County Library staff in Portland, Oregon, for assisting me in my research and for processing my many requests for resources for the last year. I'd also like to thank Bishop Museum Library and Hawaii State Library in Honolulu for research assistance and materials related to the Goddess Pele for the Hawaiian StoryImage Programs.

I thank my friends and colleagues for their continuous interest and support during the writing process.

Introduction

Do stories *move* you? What do they make you *feel?* And what do they make you want to *do?* This activity guide will enable you and the children you work and play with to creatively express and interpret imagery through the medium of movement. It is designed for librarians, teachers, parents, and caregivers. Even though the contents also support the work of dancers and storytellers, no prior experience in dance or storytelling is necessary—just the willingness to exercise your imagination!

Imagery is present everywhere in our lives: in our environment and in everything we do and perceive. It is the building block of literature. Literary images stir up our perceptions of how characters, settings, and scenes look, sound, feel, smell, taste, and *move*, our kinesthetic sense. Through movement we release energy that builds up in our muscles as we creatively respond to what we perceive.

Organization of This Guide

This guide is divided into six chapters. Each has an introduction and programs for a particular age group. You may wish to adapt a program, or use it as is, for a different age group, depending on your group's interests and capabilities. The programs lend themselves to expansion. Those in the first four chapters are "happenings" filled with images from literature and music that incite recollections of how special occasions and places in our lives looked, felt, sounded, tasted, smelled, and moved. Most likely you'll think of additional stories, poems, songs, rhymes, instrumental music, and sounds to complement and enhance the memory or mental pictures of your experience, to share with the children. The first three chapters integrate movement with a variety of literature, under the heading "Story and Movement Time." Beginning in chapter 4, vocal and movement exercises follow a story presentation and provide opportunities for children to develop storytelling skills. The chapter introductions provide an idea of how the programs address the typical cognitive and physical abilities of children in an age group. The levels of literacy (reading, writing, and speaking) and movement skills progress according to the developmental stage or readiness of the child. Each program begins with a summary of the theme and activities. Following this description are lists of books, music, space needs, and equipment and materials, followed by a list of things to do "Before You Begin." All programs have an introduction for the participants, which may include some content orientation activities. Some programs contain a craft project.

Program Content

Within these programs you and the children will be engaged in literature, music, and dances from many cultures, traditions, and styles. In the "Jiggles and Jingles Infant" programs you will find nursery rhymes, songs, games, and guided partner/group dances. Babies dance with adults; everyone participates in the program. Each infant program ends with a lullaby. In "Dancing Rhymes," toddlers are busily involved in free-form movement, using major muscle groups as they dance and learn verbs and prepositions in nursery rhymes, stories, and poems, and ride the Boogaloo Train. Preschoolers dance about to stories, funny poetry, and singing games, as they go to the circus and swim with the dolphins. They build a vocabulary of adverbs by modifying how they move. In the "StoryTrip" chapter, resources include a story from Mexico and the Mexican Hat Dance, a story from Japan and a Kabuki Onnegata (female) movement style, a story from Ghana and a celebratory funeral dance, and a story from India and a bit of yoga. Transliterated vocabulary lists and customs from other countries are included. These programs develop the children's cultural literacy. Most of the programs also include movement improvisations based on literary imagery. You will also find songs and charades.

In the more advanced programs, StoryImage™ and "Moving Stories," children learn how to interpret character, setting, and event imagery. Their voices become the music that accompanies their movements. The StoryImage program draws from both the Hawaiian culture and the growth cycle of trees. Students make two-dimensional illustrations on paper and in space with their bodies. Shapes infused with mood are conveyed in the images that the children interpret. In "Moving Stories" the oldest group of children learns how to abstract energy qualities, such as gliding, floating, pressing, dragging, dabbing, flicking, and slashing, by associating these qualities with the mood in the character, setting, and event imagery and then aligning their movement and speech to convey vivid images. See the list "Dancing Parts of Speech" in the appendix. These words and related movement simultaneously build the children's verbal and nonverbal vocabulary throughout this guide.

If you do not have a background in storytelling and wish to perform the literature, see the "Trigger Method of Learning a Story (Group Leader)" handout at the end of chapter 6.

In addition to the nursery rhymes, traditional singing games, and "The Old Lady Who Swallowed the Fly," many of the programs contain thematic poems that I wrote for the book.

Emergent Literacy and Stages of Development

Following the introduction in each chapter is a "Readiness to Learn" table. By the time most children reach the age specified in each table, they are ready to acquire the skills that enable them to partake in the activities in this guide. The information in these tables has been compiled from a number of sources (American Academy of Pediatrics 1998; Laban 1975; Shore 1997; Bybee and Sund 1982). The tables in the first three chapters, for infants, toddlers, and preschoolers, contain a section on emergent literacy abilities. The programs in these chapters are designed to draw on the young child's readiness to learn literacy-related skills. Research has shown that children display speaking and reading-related behaviors from the time that they are infants. It has been found that this early training for young children has an impact on their success not only when they enter school, but throughout their lives. A young child has a large quantity of neurons capable of creating new synapses; if these neurons are not stimulated, they die off and potential pathways of new knowledge are lost. It is important to tap these readiness capabilities of young children during this window of accelerated learning (Shore 1997). Early literacy data for the tables was derived from studies and brochures produced by The Early Literacy Project, A Partnership Among the Public Library Association, The Association for Library Service to Children, and The National Institute of Child Health & Human Development. The information in the brochures was created by Dr. Grover (Russ) Whitehurst, leading professor of psychology, State University of New York, and Dr. Christopher Lonigan, associate professor of psychology, Florida State University. The brochures can be found at http://www.ala.org/ala/pla/plaissues/earlylit/ parentguidebrochures/ parentguide.htm.

Whole Child Development

Studies indicate that children have strong responses to stories. Educator Michael Benton noted that a reader participates actively when engrossed in a story; that all actions, roles, emotional conditions, and relationships are imaginatively experienced and elaborated on by the reader. He states that, "what is going on in the child's head as he reads a story is dependent more upon what the reader brings than upon what the text offers" (Benton 1979, 72). He suggests that the reader actually remakes the story and generates a new dimension for it in his own imagination. According to dance instructor Geraldine Dimondstein, "children do not passively receive sensory impressions; they deepen and clarify what they perceive by imitating or responding in some physical way to what they see, hear, touch, or feel" (1971, 10).

Imaginative movement experiences are vital to the growth of whole and healthy human beings; they counteract the left-brain-dominated thinking produced by sedentary educational and work environments. Noted movement specialist Rudolf Laban developed a system of movement to develop the whole person. A part of this system is explored in the use of energy qualities in the "Moving Stories" chapter. According to Laban, his system creates "a poise of personality which today is often lacking because of the lop-sided development of the intellectual faculty, contrasted only with a rough-and-ready impetuosity of movement or with exaggerated self-consciousness and rigidity (1975, 49). Movement is a central part of the learning experience; it facilitates thinking. Developmental biologist, Charles Piaget's found

> that the young child attributes life to activity and this activity facilitates his thinking ability and learning. The child then begins to be aware that movement is the essence of things around him, and he discovers himself through movement.
>
> A child, like an animal, is born with a natural drive for movement and he gradually expands his own growth through the cultivation and refinement of these inner impulses until they become so internalized that he also begins to think as he moves. The child then is developing not only through the psychomotor domain, but also through the affective and cognitive domain. (Fleming 1973, 41)

Without movement to integrate subject matter, the child may develop a learning disability. "Each stage in our development of mobility corresponds to the development of an area in our brains. Our brains cannot develop properly without movement—the two are inextricably linked. Movement affects our ability to see, hear, feel, use our hands, understand and use language, and even our ability to read, think, and organize information" (Landalf and Gerke 1996, 1). Using movement with literature is a form of active learning that develops the whole child.

The arrangement of the chapters in this guide is designed to progressively expand the child's cognition, self-awareness, range of verbal and movement expression, and aesthetic sensibilities. It is my hope that the activities in this guide will pave the way to eloquence and grace for all who participate.

Chapter 1

Jiggles and Jingles Programs for Babies: Pre-Walkers

Introduction

The "Jiggles and Jingles" programs communicate with the baby through the senses of touch, sound, and sight. These literary-based programs encourage feeling, listening, seeing, and responding. Activities are designed to promote early literacy as they simultaneously open and expand limbs and develop eye/hand coordination. The baby's abilities to grasp, gather, open and close hands, pull, touch, move, shake things, kick, stretch, crawl, roll over, scoot, bounce, and repeat actions are expanded in simple and fun movement exercises.

As the baby interacts in the program activities, he or she is encouraged to "explore" books. Early literacy skills are built through playing with books, being read to, having objects pointed out in the books, hearing new words, watching words form from the speaker's mouth, responding to questions, and "conversing" (babbling, cooing, and other sounds) with the reader.

The combination of movement and literature develops the abundance of neural connections in the baby's brain. The repetition of sounds and movement and a variety of vocal intonations and rhythms encourage the language, listening, observation, imaginative, and movement skills of the baby. A baby, when awake, is in constant motion, full of babbles, with all the senses ready to match words with actions.

These programs are thematic to engage parents or caregivers, which in turn will engage the babies. Babies learn from and enjoy watching, listening to, and imitating what their significant adults and older children do and say. Details about babies' cognitive, physical, and emergent literacy skills are outlined in Table 1.1.

Table 1.1. Readiness to Learn (Babies/Non-Walkers)

COGNITIVE	PHYSICAL	LITERACY BUILDING
➤ Reacts to stimuli in environment ➤ Perceives through 5 senses ➤ Seeks hidden objects ➤ Experiments with cause and effect ➤ Listens, responds, imitates, and makes sounds ➤ Says first words, laughs ➤ Relates to physical objects from the literature ➤ Understands own name ➤ Understands language before can talk	➤ Sits up ➤ Uses hands and arms: grasps, gathers, opens and closes, pulls, moves things, touches, shakes objects (simple rattles and bells) ➤ Repeats actions to elicit change ➤ Uses legs and feet: kicks, plays with toes ➤ Interacts with parent/caregiver ➤ Can be made aware of playful use of shoulders, elbows, wrists, fingers, hips, knees, toes, head, chest, and back ➤ Can be encouraged in eye-hand coordination ➤ Uses whole body: stretches, crawls, rolls over, bounces, scoots ➤ Smiles	*Awareness of books:* ➤ Give books to play with and chew Engaging in book sharing: ➤ Read often to baby ➤ Point to things in book, relate to baby's life ➤ Cuddle as you read *Awareness of letters:* ➤ Feel a ball and say "The ball is round." Feel a block and say the block is square." *Learning new words:* ➤ Say new words ➤ Notice and encourage baby watching your mouth forming words ➤ Ask and answer questions, pointing to a picture or saying the answer ➤ Converse about what baby is seeing, hearing, feeling, and doing to create new synapses in baby's brain ➤ Respond to babbles or whatever baby utters; listen closely to understand what baby is trying to say *Working with literary resources:* ➤ Board books: photos of babies ➤ Familiar items, rhyme and repetition, textures, animal sounds, lullaby books songs, nursery rhymes ➤ Cloth, board, or vinyl books with few/no words *Developing speaking skills:* ➤ Talk to baby about what you are doing all day long ➤ Read favorite books again and again *Developing syllable awareness:* ➤ Sing songs for different sounds of syllables

The person presenting the program models what is to be said and done by the parents or caregivers. All babies will need a small chair with a tie or a baby car seat. Everyone dances in the "Jiggles and Jingles" program: babies and adults!

Program 1: Bathtub Ballet

Summary

Parents or caregivers actively participate in this moving story time for babies. Everybody gets to dance! In Part 1 the nursery rhyme, "Peek-a-Boo" is played as a game, read from a book, and danced to a song. Babies "explore" board books and are led in a dance that activates and gently stretches their muscles. In Part 2 babies meet Quack in the tub, in a book, in a game, and in a circle dance. The program concludes with an after bath poem and a "Mozart Lullaby." The program takes about 40 minutes.

Program Preparation

Books

Peek-a-Boo Books

- Grobel Intrater, Roberta. *Peek-a-Boo!* New York: Scholastic, 1997. Attractive color photos of captioned baby faces in a variety of expressions.

- Grobel Intrater, Roberta *Peek-a-Boo, You!* New York: Scholastic, 2002. Life-sized photos of happy baby faces with oversized lift-up flaps.

- Ormerod, Jan. *Peek-a-Boo!* New York: Dutton Children's Books, 1998. Lift the flap on babies hiding and showing their faces.

- Tuxworth, Nicola. *Peek-a-Boo.* Say and Point Picture Boards. London: Lorenz, 2004.

Other Books in the Program

- Root, Phyllis. *Quack!* Cambridge, MA: Candlewick Press, 2005. When Mama Duck calls, the newly hatched ducklings follow her and have fun on the way.

- Sheehan, Nancy. *Baby Messy, Baby Clean.* New York: Dutton Children's Books, 1999. Photographs of infants and toddlers getting messy as they explore their world, then get cleaned up at bath time.

- Board/juvenile books with pictures of ducks, for children to "explore," such as:

  – Alborough, Jez. *Duck in the Truck.* La Jolla, CA: Kane/Miller, 2005.

  – Buzzeo, Toni. *Dawdle Duckling.* New York: Dial Books for Young Readers, 2003.

  – Herman, Gail. *The Littlest Duckling.* New York: Viking, 1996.

    – Kitamura, Satoshi. *Pato está sucio.* Mexico City: Fondo de Cultura Económica, 1998.

    – Tafuri, Nancy. *Goodnight, My Duckling.* New York: Scholastic, 2006.

    – Thompson, Lauren. *Little Quack's Hide and Seek.* New York: Simon & Schuster Books for Young Readers, 2004.

- Board/juvenile books with pictures of babies, for babies to "explore," such as:

    – Asquith, Ros. *Babies.* New York: Simon & Schuster Books for Young Readers, 2003.

    – Cowen-Fletcher, Jane. *Baby Angels.* Cambridge, MA: Candlewick Press, 1997, 1996.

Music

- Dines, Katherine. Adaptation of traditional "Peek-a-Boo" song from *Hunk-Ta, Bunk-TA Funsies 1.* Denver: Hunk-Ta, Bunk-TA Music, 2003; or

- Finck, Terri Thurman. "Mozart Lullaby" from *Galliump Lullabies.* Klamath Falls, OR: Kid-Tunes, 2002.

- Hap, Palmer. *Peek-a-Boo and Other Songs for Young Children.* Topanga, CA: Hap-Pal Music, 1997; and

- Kaye, Danny. "Ugly Duckling" song from *A Child's Celebration of Song.* Redway, CA: Music for Little People, 1992.

Space Needs

- A carpeted space about 20 by 20 feet, for 16 adults and babies sitting in a circle.

Materials and Equipment

- CD and cassette player

- Lightweight washcloth for each baby

- Plastic duck for each baby

- One baby-sized baby doll for demonstration

- Two board books for each attendee, preferably one with a picture of a baby and one with a picture of a duck

- Several board, cloth, or vinyl books for babies to explore.

- Car seats, brought by parents or caregivers

- Small chairs with scarves or ties on which to seat babies who don't have a car seat

- Handouts: rhymes included at end of this section (enlarge as needed)

- Two metal or plastic stands to hold rhymes enlarged to 8½ by 11 inches

Before You Begin

- Gather or purchase and set up all materials and equipment.
- Make two enlarged copies of rhymes to display on stands on both sides of you for participants to say with you as you do the program.
- Read over and practice the words and movements in the program.

Program

Introduction

> Welcome to "Bathtub Ballet." This program is an easy and fun way to introduce your baby to literature and creative dance. The activities will pave the way for your baby to read, listen, speak, and write, and to move gracefully. Please repeat what I say directly to your baby and do what I do with Cindy, my baby doll.

You may choose another name for your doll. Have everyone sit in a circle. Sitting parents or caregivers will be facing their babies, with the babies sitting in car seats or in small chairs, to their front or side.

Story and Movement Time

Part 1: Peek-a-Boo (15 Minutes)

Leader: *But first we must find the BABY. Where's the BABY? You can substitute your own baby's name: Where is Cindy?* [Place your demo doll in a car seat and use it to demonstrate the program.]

Peek-a-Boo (traditional rhyme)

> **Movement***:* Place your palms over your eyes, hiding your eyes.
>
> **1. Leader:** *Peek-a-Boo*
>
> **Movement:** Uncover your eyes.
>
> **2. Leader:** *I See You*
>
> Repeat.
>
> **Movement:** Hold the baby's hands over the baby's eyes.
>
> **3. Leader:** *Peek-a-Boo*
>
> **Movement:** Uncover the baby's eyes.

4. Leader: *I See You*

Repeat.

Have everyone place their babies in their laps, facing you as you walk around the inside of the circle, showing the pictures and reading one of the peek-a-boo books. Direct the words and pictures toward each baby as you pass by.

Baby Improv

Play one of the musical versions of "Peek-a-Boo." Place the pile of board books in the center of the circle. While the music is playing, let the babies play with the books and move around and then: Have the parents sing with you to their babies what they are doing in the following movement.

Leader: *Gliding baby's arms to and fro, to and fro, to and fro. Lifting baby up and down, up and down, up and down, jumping off the ground, off the ground, off the ground. Gently stretching babies' arms to the side and up over their heads. Whew! On your back I wiggle and gently stretch your legs.* [Put books away to make room for the upcoming Ugly Duckling Circle Dance.]

Up we go! [Have parents pick up babies and sit them on their laps facing the center of the circle.]

Part 2: Quack (25 Minutes)

Read the book *Baby Messy, Baby Clean*. Walk around the inside of the circle, showing the babies the pictures. Have everyone put their babies back in their seats.

Leader: *Let's pretend we're taking a morning bath.* [Give all the adults a washcloth and remind them to copy what you do and repeat what you say, as you recite the poem.]

Rub a Dub Dub (adaptation of the traditional version)

1. Leader: *Rub a Dub Dub*

Movement: Have adults wash arms with washcloths.

2. Leader: *Rub a Dub Dub*

Movement: Have adults wash babies' arms with washcloths.

3. Leader: *Three are in this tub. One, Two, Three!*

Movement: Count numbers slowly as you raise your fingers one by one.

4. Leader: *Who could they be?*

Movement: Tilt your head side to side, with a wondering look.

5. Leader: *Baby*

Movement: Tap the baby on the chest.

6. Leader: *Ducky; where is Ducky?*

Movement: Tilt your head side to side, with a wondering look.

7. Leader: *And Me!*

Movement: Tap yourself on the chest.

8. Leader: *Quack! Quack! Quack! Where is that Ducky?*

Have everyone place their babies in their laps, facing you as you walk around the inside of the circle. Direct the words and pictures toward each baby as you pass by, and then place a duck behind each parent's or caregiver's back.

Read the book *Quack.*

Lucky Ducky (original poem)

Where is that ducky? Play hide and seek with the ducks: Have the parents hide them and then show them and hide them again. Finally, have the adults put the ducks next to their faces and mimic what you say and do.

1. Leader: *He's feeling very Mucky, this Ducky!*

Movement: Hold the ducky close to your face and make a very sad expression.

2. Leader: *So, he ran away, this Mucky Duck*

Movement: Move the ducky in the air to the left in a bouncy motion.

3. Leader: *He found a lake to swim upon*

Movement: Place the ducky on the raised palm of your hand.

4. Leader: *He was now a Lucky Ducky*

Movement: Glide your hand back and forth in a swimming motion and give the ducky to the baby.

5. Leader: *So lucky was he, that by dawn he was a beautiful swan*

Movement: Flap your arms gracefully, gradually raising them.

Ugly Duckling Circle Dance

Have the parents or caregivers pick up the babies and gather in the center of room. Have the adults say the following several times, with you and to each other, in the group: *You're ugly; nobody likes you!*

Play "The Ugly Duckling" song by Danny Kaye. Quoted phrases below are words in the song that everyone can sing along with.

1. Leader: *Sad duckling runs and hides from the beginning of the music to the following words in the song: "Till a flock of swan spied him there . . . you're a very fine swan indeed."*

Movement: Run and huddle with the baby to the corners or sides of room. Repeat several times to other parts of the room. Gather everyone into a circle, facing the center of the circle, arms' length apart.

2. Leader: *"Me a swan?"*

Movement: See your reflection in the water: Swoop the baby down and look into the imaginary lake.

I Am a Swan.

Repeat.

3. Leader: *"I'm not such an Ugly Duckling."*

Movement: Walk counterclockwise in circle, balancing the baby on your tummy as you walk.

4. Leader: *"And a head so noble and high."*

Movement: Raise the baby overhead and twirl around in place.

5. Leader: *"I am a swan!"*

Have the parents or caregivers hold their babies on their laps with their duckies for the following poem. As before, have them do what you do and repeat each line to their babies as you say it:

Clean and Sweet (original poem)

　　　1. Leader: *Now baby is clean and sweet*

　　Movement: Smell the baby's sweetness.

　　　2. Leader: *Bathed in the glow of love*

　　Movement: Look in the baby's eyes and give him or her a big hug.

3. Leader: *Shining face and shining feet*

Movement: Touch the baby's face and feet.

4. Leader: *A duckling, you did meet*

Movement: Hold up the ducky.

5. Leader: *Or was it a swan? Yes, YOU are the Swan. Isn't that neat?*

Movement: Swoop the baby up.

Lullaby

Rock the babies for the playing of the "Mozart Lullaby."

Rub a Dub Dub

Rub a Dub Dub

Rub a Dub Dub; Three are in this Tub

One, Two, Three!

Who could they be?

Baby

Ducky; where is Ducky?

And Me!

Quack! Quack! Quack! Where is that Ducky?

Lucky Ducky

He's feeling very Mucky, this Ducky!

So, he ran away, this Mucky Duck

He found a lake to swim upon

He was now a Lucky Ducky

So lucky was he, that by dawn he was a Beautiful Swan

Clean and Sweet

Now baby is clean and sweet

Bathed in the glow of love

Shining face and shining feet

A duckling, you did meet

Or was it a swan? Yes, YOU are

the Swan.

Isn't that neat?

Program 2: Going to Town

Summary

Parents or caregivers actively participate in this moving story time for babies. Everybody gets to move! In Part 1 the baby is greeted with a song and a moving poem. In Part 2 the baby takes a trip to London Town to go to the market. On the way the baby meets cows in the meadow, where everyone plays Peek-a-Moo and does the Buzzing Bee Dance. In Part 3, in town, at the market, a fat pig and a Plum Pat-a-Cake are purchased. In Part 4 the return home at the end of a busy, buzzy day is made at a snail's pace, and the program concludes with the "Rock-a-Bye Baby" lullaby. The program takes about one hour.

Program Preparation

Books

Peek-a-Moo Books

- Cimarusti, Marie Torres. *Peek-a-Moo*. Illustrated by Stephanie Peterson. New York: Dutton's Children's Books, 1998. All the animals and a baby play peek-a-boo. Lift-up flaps show the hands of each one.

- Most, Bernard. *Peek-a-Moo*. San Diego: Harcourt Brace, 1998. A playful calf plays the peek-a-boo game with the other animals and the farmer.

Other Program Books

- Wallace, Karen. *Busy, Buzzy Bee*. New York: DK Publishing, 1999. Explains the behavior and lives of bees, discussing how they collect nectar from flowers, care for their eggs and the queen bee, and communicate with each other. Good pictures of bees.

- Pat-a-cake books

  – Collins, Heather. *Pat-a-Cake*. Tonawanda, NY: Kids Can Press, 2003.

  – Kenyon, Tony. *Pat-a-Cake*. Cambridge, MA: Candlewick Press, 1998.

- Books with cow pictures and other board books for baby to "explore," such as: Blackstone, Stella. *There's a Cow in the Cabbage Patch*. Cambridge, MA: Barefoot Books, 2002.

- If possible, also include the following book: Gentieu, Penny. *Baby! Talk!* New York: Crown Publishers, 1999. Photographs and simple text present a group of babies finding their feet, playing pat-a-cake, eating, hugging, and more.

Music

- Dana, Al, et al. "Be My Baby Bumble Bee" song from *Four Baby Bumblebees.* Long Branch, NJ: Kimbo Educational, 2001.

- Sharon, Lois, and Bram. "Rock-a-Bye Baby" song from *Mainly Mother Goose.* Toronto: Elephant Records; Hollywood, CA: A&M Records, 1984.

Space Needs

- Carpeted space about 20 feet by 20 feet, for 16 adults and babies sitting in a circle.

Materials and Equipment

- CD and cassette player

- One baby-sized baby doll for demonstration

- Car seats or small chairs and scarves to tie around the babies, if the babies cannot sit up on their own (brought by parents or caregivers)

- Soft, small spongy balls for each baby

- Cow toys: figures or stuffed animals (optional)

- Handouts: rhymes included at end of this chapter (enlarge as needed)

- Two metal or plastic stands to hold rhymes enlarged to 8½ by 11 inches

Before You Begin

- Gather or purchase and set up all materials and equipment.

- Make two enlarged copies of rhymes to display on stands on both sides of you for participants to say with you as you do the program.

- Read over and practice the words and movements in the program.

Program

Introduction

> Today we are "Going to Town." This program is an easy and fun way to introduce your baby to literature and creative dance. The activities will pave the way for your baby to read, listen, speak, and write, and to move gracefully. Please repeat what I say directly to your baby and do what I do with Cindy, my baby doll.

You may choose another name for your doll. Have everyone sit in a circle. Sitting parents or caregivers will be facing their babies, with their babies sitting in car seats or in small chairs, to their front or side.

Story and Movement Time

Part 1: Greeting Baby (10 Minutes)

Leader: *First we will greet our babies.*

Good Morning Song (Sing to the tune of "Happy Birthday to You") (traditional song)

> *Good morning to you,*
>
> *Good morning to you.*
>
> *Good morning, dear* ____ [Insert baby's name.]
>
> *Good morning to you.*

Baby Face Rhyme (traditional rhyme)

> **1. Leader:** *Two little eyes*
>
> **Movement:** Blink a few times and touch your eyelids and then touch the baby's eyelids.
>
> **2. Leader:** *To see everything*
>
> **Movement:** Move your index finger, extended straight up, back and forth, and then around, in front of the baby's eyes.
>
> **3. Leader:** *Two little ears*
>
> **Movement:** Touch your ears and then the baby's ears.
>
> **4. Leader:** *To hear everything*
>
> **Movement:** Cup your ear and *buzz* in the baby's ear.
>
> **5. Leader:** *One little nose*
>
> **Movement:** Touch your nose and then touch the baby's nose.
>
> **6. Leader:** *To smell everything*
>
> **Movement:** Sniff a few times and exhale through your mouth.
>
> **7. Leader:** *One little mouth that likes to eat everything*
>
> **Movement:** Touch your mouth and then the baby's, then smack your lips and say:
>
> **8. Leader:** *Yum, Yum.* **Likes to eat!** *Then we must go to the market and buy some* **FOOD**. *Let's go shopping in LONDON TOWN!*

Part 2: Trip Time (25 Minutes)

In a jazzy tone, sing out the following:

1. Leader: *Every baby get ready*

Movement: Gently move the baby's arms out to the side and then in front of the baby's body, back a forth, a few times.

2. Leader: *'Cause we're going to TOWN*

Movement: Untie the band around the baby or take the baby out of the car seat and lift the baby up into the air.

Lower and lift the baby again.

Seat the baby on your lap; the baby should be facing the inside of the room, with his or her back to you.

3. Leader: *One foot up and the other down*

Movement: Walk the baby or lift each leg.

4. Leader: *This is the way to London Town*

Repeat.

Read or show the pictures in *Busy, Buzzy Bee.* Walk around the inside of the circle, and show each baby a picture.

Read one of the "peek-a-moo" books. Walk around the inside of the circle and show each baby a picture.

1. Leader: *Now we're on our way, with two little eyes to look around*

Movement: Place board books with pictures of cows in the center of the room. Move your index finger back and forth in front of the baby's eyes and point to the meadow, cow, cow toys, and other board books in the center of the circle.

2. Leader: *Oh, what do we see in the meadow? Five Little Cows*

Movement: Move with the baby to be near the center of the circle, near the board books and other babies. Let them "explore" the books.

Cows in the Meadow (original rhyme)

1. Leader: *This cow eats grass*

This cow eats oats

This cow drinks from the trough

This cow swats a fly

This cow does nothing—

Movement: Touch each of the baby's fingers as you mention each cow.

2. Leader: *Just sleeps all day long*

Movement: Fall backward with the baby.

Repeat on the other hand.

Leader: *Lazy cow, let's get up and* **give her a BUZZ!**

Buzzing Bee Dance

Parents or caregivers get up with the babies and dance around "the meadow" to the "Be My Baby Bumble Bee" song. Have half the couples (baby and parent or caregiver) be the cows, lumbering lazily around the room, saying "Moo, Moo." The other half should chase them, saying "BZZZZ, BZZZZ." Then change roles.

Part 3: At the Market (15 Minutes)

Have everyone sit back down and place the babies on their knees.

Leader: *We are about to arrive at the market!*

To Market, to Market (adapted from the traditional rhyme)

1. Leader: *To market, to market*

Movement: Place the baby on your lap.

2. Leader: *To buy a fat pig. Home again, home again*

Movement: Bend your knees, place the baby on them, and gently move your knees up and down, while holding the baby's arms.

3. Leader: *Jiggety-jig*

Movement: Unbend your knees and straighten your legs. Bounce the baby in your lap. Then bend your knees and place the baby on them and gently bounce the baby.

4. Leader: *To market, to market. Going by the lake, there is the Baker ready to bake a plum cake.*

Repeat.

Leader: *Place your babies on your laps, facing the inside of the circle.*

Read one of the "pat-a-cake" books. Go around the inside of the circle, showing the pictures to the babies.

Leader: *Place your baby facing you in the chair, or put the baby back in the car seat.*

Pat-a-Cake (traditional rhyme)

> **Leader:** *Let's play Pat-a-Cake.*

1. Leader: *Pat-a-cake,*

Movement: Clap your hands together.

2. Leader: *Pat-a-cake,*

Movement: Clap the baby's hands together.

3. Leader: *Baker's man,*

Movement: Clap the baby's right hand with your right hand and the baby's left hand with your left hand.

4. Leader: *Bake me a cake*

Movement: Cup the baby's hands in your hands.

5. Leader: *As fast as you can.*

Movement: Shake the baby's cupped hands.

6. Leader: *Pat it and prick it*

Movement: Pat the baby's right hand with your right hand and the baby's left hand with your left hand.

7. Leader: *And mark it with B,*

Movement: Write a "B" with your index finger on the baby's palm.

8. Leader: *And put it in the oven*

Movement: Cup the baby's hands in your hands.

9. Leader: *For Baby and me*

Movement: Give the baby a hug.

10. Leader: *Write a "B" with your index finger on the baby's palm, as you say "B" is for Baby.*

Movement: Touch the baby on the chest.

11. Leader: *Write a "B" with your finger on the baby's palm, as you say "B" is for Bumblebee.*

Movement: Point to the picture of the Bumblebee on the cover of *Busy, Buzzy Bee,* and repeat the phrase as you take it around and show it to all the babies.

12. Leader: *Write a "B" with your finger on the baby's palm, as you say "B" is for Ball.*

Movement: Give each baby a soft ball to squeeze.

Part 4: Going Home by Snail and Lullaby (5 Minutes)

Leader: *Yawn: Oh, I'm tired; let's go home; let's take the snail home.*

The Snail Ride (original poem)

1. Leader: *Slowly, Slowly, Going Home*

Movement: Walk your fingers over the baby's shoulders and down the baby's back.

2. Leader: *On the back of a snail. Slowly, going up, over the rail.*

Movement: Walk your fingers over the baby's shoulder and down the baby's arm.

3. Leader: [Yawn] *Umm, tomorrow we shall have a delicious baked ham and plum cake, Yum, Yum.*

Movement: Tickle the baby's tummy.

4. Leader: *But now it is late and time to go to sleep.*

Play "Rock-a-Bye Baby."

Everyone rocks their babies in their arms to the music.

Baby Face Rhyme

Two little eyes

To see everything

Two little ears

To hear everything

One little nose

To smell everything

One little mouth that likes to eat everything

Yum, Yum. Likes to Eat! Then we must go to the market and buy some FOOD. Let's go shopping in LONDON TOWN!

Baby Hand Rhyme

This cow eats grass

This cow eats oats

This cow drinks from the trough

This cow swats a fly

This cow does nothing—

Just sleeps all day long

(Repeat on other hand.)

Lazy cow, let's get up and give her a BUZZ!

Pat-a-Cake

Pat-a-cake,

Pat-a-cake,

Baker's man,

Bake me a cake

As fast as you can.

Pat it and prick it

And mark it with B,

And put it in the oven

For Baby and me

Chapter 2

Dancing Rhymes Programs for Toddlers: Walkers

Introduction

The "Dancing Rhymes" programs draw the attention of the active toddler through the medium of lively nursery rhymes, rhythmic poems, and songs along with basic large muscle and repetitive movement. There's lots of room for spontaneity of movement and speech to encourage learning. Activities are designed to promote early literacy as they simultaneously build muscle and mind-body coordination and vocabulary. Toddlers when awake are in constant motion, full of new words and phrases, and ready to show you how and where they can move. Dancing verbs and prepositions are in the forefront, as the child jumps, climbs, pushes, and pulls his or her way in, on, up, and around objects from the literary imagery.

As the toddler interacts in the program activities, he or she is encouraged to "explore" books. Early literacy skills are built through turning the pages of books, being read to, having objects pointed out in the books, hearing new words, "writing," and responding to "what" questions during reading.

The combination of movement and literature develops the abundance of neural connections in the toddler's brain. The repetition of sounds and movement and a variety of vocal intonations and rhythms encourage the language, listening, observation, imaginative, and movement skills of the toddler. Details about toddlers' cognitive, physical, and emergent literacy skills are outlined in Table 2.1.

Table 2.1. Readiness to Learn (Toddlers/Walkers)

COGNITIVE	PHYSICAL	LITERACY BUILDING
➢ Learns many new words, short sentences ➢ Responds to suggestions ➢ Exhibits reading-like and writing-like behavior ➢ Engages in some social play ➢ Identifies objects ➢ Asks simple questions	➢ Simple motor play, large muscle movement ➢ Spontaneous, repetitive movement ➢ Whole body, both legs, both arms together ➢ Active movements: jumps, beats arms, climbs, pulls, pushes ➢ Quick actions ➢ Free form; responds to suggested movement in own way ➢ Enjoys moving freely to music ➢ Finger dexterity ➢ Gaining body control	*Awareness of books:* ➢ Read aloud every day to toddler: books, labels, signs ➢ Let child hold the book and turn pages *Engage in book sharing:* ➢ Have fun reading anywhere ➢ Provide materials for pretend writing ➢ Read favorite book many times *Encourage awareness of letters:* ➢ Feel a ball and say, "The ball is round." Feel a block and say, "The block is square." Talk about the difference between the two. Compare to letter shapes. ➢ Have the child handle magnetic, felt, clay, or cookie shapes and letters. *Teach new words:* ➢ The child points to pictures to identify new words. ➢ The child answers "what" questions related to story content. ➢ The child learns from what the speaker adds to child's answer. ➢ The child watches letters being drawn. ➢ The speaker and child read together every day, adding details to the reading as the child talks about the book. *Work with literary resources:* ➢ Small picture books that they can hold ➢ Simple rhymes ➢ Familiar items (shoes, toys, pets) ➢ Familiar routines (bed, bath, meals) ➢ Lift-the-flap books ➢ Few and repeating words ➢ Goodnight books ➢ Simple alphabet books, songs *Develop speaking skills:* ➢ Dialogue or conversation about the books that you are sharing with them *Develop syllable awareness:* ➢ Read books that rhyme. ➢ Say nursery rhymes and make your own silly rhymes.

These programs are thematic to engage parents or caregivers, which in turn will engage the toddler. Toddlers learn from and enjoy watching, listening to, and imitating what their significant adults do and say. The person presenting the program models what is to be said and done by the parents or caregivers. Everyone dances in the toddler programs: toddlers and adults!

Program 1: Growing Toward the Sun

Summary

The children participate in moving activities from imagery in books, poems, and stories about the growth cycle, from seed to tree and full-grown sunflowers. Seeds are planted, nourished by rain and sun, sprouted, and matured as they are enjoyed by the growing children. Easy-to-make stick rain and sunflower stick puppets can be used in the dances; patterns are included. The program takes about 45 minutes.

Program Preparation

Books

Seed Stories

- Hall, Zoe. *The Surprise Garden*. Illustrated by Shari Halpern. New York: Blue Sky Press, 1998. After sowing unmarked seeds, three youngsters wait expectantly for their garden to grow. They grow vegetables and a sunflower.

- Hutchins, Pat, *Titch*. New York: Macmillan, 1971. Nothing Titch owned amounted to much, except the smallest thing of all—a seed.

Tree Books

- DePalma, Mary Newell. *A Grand Old Tree*. New York: A.A. Levine Books, 2005. A book about the life of a tree and all it gives us.

- Udry, Janice May. *A Tree Is Nice*. Illustrated by Marc Simont. New York: Harper, 1956. Briefly describes the value of a tree.

Flower Book

- Wellington, Monica. *Zinnia's Flower Garden*. New York: Dutton Children's Books, 2005. Zinnia plants a garden, eagerly waits for the plants to grow, sells the beautiful flowers, then gathers seeds to plant the following year.

Rain Books

- Appelt, Kathi. *Rain Dance*. Illustrated by Emilie Chollat. [New York]: HarperFestival, 2001.

- Martin, Bill, Jr., and John Archambaul. *Listen to the Rain.* Illustrated by James Endicott. New York: Henry. Holt 1988. This book describes the changing sounds of the rain: the slow soft sprinkle, the drip-drop tinkle, the sounding pounding roaring, and the fresh wet silent after-time.

- Tresselt, Alvin. *Rain Drop Splash.* Illustrated by Leonard Weisgard. New York: Lothrop, Lee & Shepard, 1946. The rain came all day and made a puddle, which grew to be a pond, which spilled over into a lake, which grew to be a river and finally joined the sea.

Music

- "Here Comes the Sun," from *All You Need Is Love: [Beatles Songs for Kids].* Redway, CA: Music for Little People, 1999; or

- Beatles. *"Here Comes the Sun,"* from *Abbey Road.* Parlophone, 1969.

- "Rain Falling," from *Hush Little Baby: Soothing Sounds for Sleep.* Pacific Palisades, CA: Kids Music Factory, 2000.

- "Goodbye Song," from *Mommy & Me: Playgroup Favorites.* Beverly Hills, CA: Concord, 2004.

- Muldaur, Maria. "The Garden Song," from *A Child's Celebration of Song.* Redway, CA: Music for Little People, 1992.

Space Needs

- Carpeted or smooth movement space, about 20 feet by 20 feet, for 20 toddlers and adults.

Materials and Equipment

- CD and cassette player

- Large umbrella

- Pictures of a tree seedling and a full-grown tree

- Large pot filled with soil and hulled sunflower seeds

- Very small plastic cups to water the seeds

- For stick puppets: three straws for two puppets for each child; yellow bond or poster paper, one 8½-by-11-inch page for every two children (to make two sunflower puppets per page); 6-by-5-inch pieces of tin foil for each child for rain puppets

- Thick flat stick, 2-inch tape for sunflower puppets

- Glue for rain puppets

- Handouts: rhymes included at end of this section (enlarge as needed)

- Two metal/plastic stands to hold enlarged rhymes

Before You Begin

- Gather or purchase and set up all materials and equipment.

- Make two enlarged copies of rhymes to display on stands on both sides of you for participants to say with you as you do the program.

- Read over and practice the words and movements in the program.

- Make rain and sunflower stick puppets, one for each child (templates and instructions in figures 2.1 and 2.2).

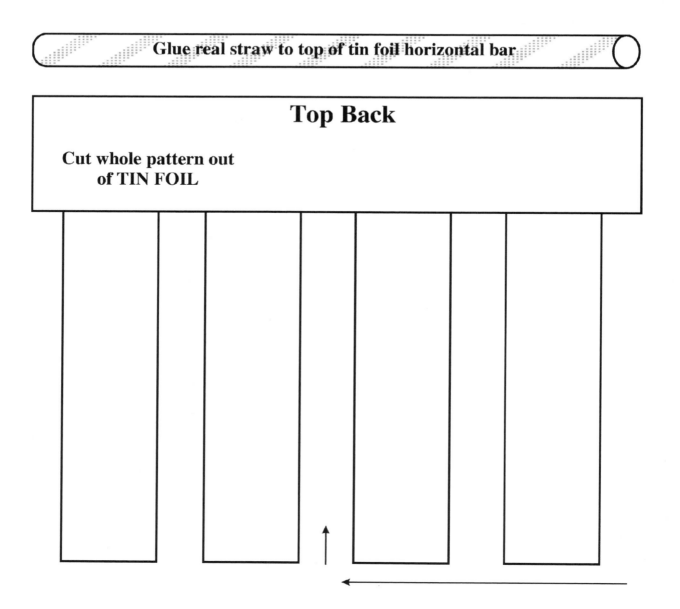

Glue real straw to top of tin foil horizontal bar

Top Back

**Cut whole pattern out
 of TIN FOIL**

1. Cut out the pattern and attach to tin foil with pins. Cut a stack of tin foil sheets at the same time to save cutting each one separately.

2. Outline the pattern on tin foil.

3. Cut out the rain puppets from the tin foil.

4. Glue one straw to top bar and the other perpendicular to it for the handle.

5. Trim straw as needed to fit tin foil. Use real straws, not drawn straws.

Figure 2.1. Rain Stick Puppet.

Use a real straw

1. Cut out the pattern and attach it to heavy yellow bond or poster board paper with straight pins. Cut several pages at once to avoid cutting each one separately.

2. Outline the pattern on the paper.

3. Cut out the sunflower puppets.

4. Attach a straw with heavy tape about 2 inches wide. Trim the straw if needed.

Figure 2.2. Sunflower Stick Puppet.

Program

Introduction

> Our story time today is called "Growing Toward the Sun." This program is an easy and fun way to introduce your toddler to literature and creative dance. The activities will pave the way for your child to read, listen, speak, and write, and to move gracefully. Through stories and rhymes we will re-create the growth of seeds into trees and blossoming sunflowers.

Story and Movement Time

Part 1: Greeting (5 Minutes)

In a sing-song voice, using no particular melody, sing the following:

Good Morning to You! (traditional rhyme)

> **Leader:** *Good morning to you!*
>
> *Good morning to you!*
>
> *We're all in our places*
>
> *With bright, shining faces.*
>
> *Oh, this is the way to start a great day!*
>
> *"Are you ready for a great day?"*
>
> [Give them time to respond to develop their language skills.]

Part 2: Planting Seeds (15 Minutes)

Read and show pictures from one or more of the seed books.

Leader: *Every day you are growing bigger and bigger, aren't you? Trees grow bigger and bigger every day, too. Here is a baby tree.* [Show them the pictures of the seedling.] *And here is a full-grown tree.* [Show them the picture of the mature tree.] *Just like you, trees grow from tiny seeds. Let's be tiny seeds all curled up tight.*

Tiny Seeds (original poem)

> **1. Leader:** *Tiny seeds all curled up tight*
>
> **Movement:** Curl up your body on the floor in the form of a seed.
>
> **2. Leader:** *Sound asleep; its night, night*
>
> **Movement:** Remain still.

3. Leader: *Rain splashes all around*

Movement: Raise up, sitting on your heels, your hands making a splashing down motion.

4. Leader: *The sun comes up and warms the ground*

Movement: Still sitting, raise your arms gradually and then lower them, palms down, swinging them slowly in a low arc in front of your knees.

5. Leader: *Tiny seeds shoot out your roots*

Movement: Stretch your legs and bend your knees to one side.

6. Leader: *A lovely tree, for all to see*

Movement: Rise onto your knees and stand up tall, then stretch up, open your arms wide to the sides and rotate your body left to right, then right to left.

Read and show pictures from *A Tree Is Nice.*

Leader: *Flowers come from seeds, too.* [Read and show the pictures from *Zinnia's Flower Garden.*]

Planting a Sunflower Seed (original rhyme)

[Get out the large pot and the sunflower seeds.]

1. Leader: *Today, let's plant a sunflower*

Movement: Plant a seed, and have each child put a seed in the dirt.

2. Leader: *We know just how to cover the seed most carefully*

Movement: Press the dirt around the seeds, with everyone helping.

3. Leader: *We know just how to cover the seed most carefully*

Movement: Stand and dance joyfully, turning and pressing your hands down to indicate covering the seed.

4. Leader: *It's only a baby now*

Movement: Pretend you are rocking a baby in your arms.

5. Leader: *Each day it will grow and grow*

For all to see

Movement: With your arms out in front of you, elbows slightly bent, palms facing you, slide one palm up from behind the other palm and splay the fingers on the inside hand. The image is a sunflower sprouting and opening.

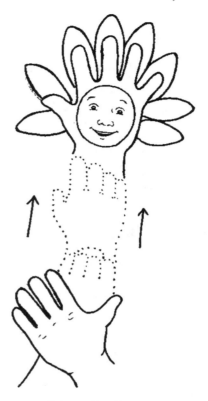

I Am a Sunflower.

7. Leader: *Hour after hour, as we know, the seed will grow into a beautiful sunflower*

Movement: Smile and frame your face with your hands, the tips of your thumbs touching your cheeks and your palms splayed out.

Part 3: Nourishing the Seeds (15 Minutes)

Play "The Garden Song" as background music for the next activity.

Leader: [Give each child a small cup of water to water the seeds.] *We are feeding the seeds so they will grow.* [Read and show pictures from one of the rain books.] *Now the rain is feeding the seeds.* [Play the "Rain Falling" song. Pull out and open the large umbrella and invite the children to join you under the umbrella. Let the children shake the tinfoil puppets as they listen to the rain. Lower the sound on the tape and recite the following:]

It's Raining; It's Pouring (traditional rhyme)

Leader: *It's raining, it's pouring;*

The old man is snoring.

He bumped his head

And went to bed

And couldn't get up in the morning.

Rain, rain, go away;

Come again another day;

We want to go out and play.

[Repeat, and encourage children and adults to sing with you.]

Leader: *Now the sun is feeding the seeds.*

Sunflower Dance

Play "Here Comes the Sun" song. Give the children the sunflower stick puppets to hold up as they dance freely to the music.

Part 4: Harvest Celebration and Parting (10 Minutes)

Harvest Hoedown

Sing the following:

If You're Happy and You Know It (traditional song)

1. Leader: *We have gathered our beautiful sunflowers. I'm very happy; are you? If you're happy and you know it, clap your hands.*

Movement: Clap your hands three times.

2. Leader: *If you're happy and you know it, clap you hands.*

Movement: Clap your hands three times.

3. Leader: *If you're happy and you know it, then your face will surely show it.*

Movement: Smile and point to your face.

4. Leader: *If you're happy and you know it, clap your hands.*

Movement: Clap your hands three times.

5. Leader: *If you're happy and you know it, stomp your feet.*

Movement: Stomp your feet three times.

6. Leader: *If you're happy and you know it, stomp your feet.*

Movement: Stomp your feet three times.

7. Leader: *If you're happy and you know it, then your face will surely show it.*

Movement: Smile and point to your face.

8. Leader: *If you're happy and you know it, stomp your feet.*

Movement: Stomp your feet three times.

Leader: *If you're happy and you know it, jump up and down.*

Movement: Jump four times.

Leader: *If you're happy and you know it, jump up and down.*

Movement: Jump four times.

Leader: *If you're happy and you know it, then your face will surely show it.*

Movement: Smile and point to your face.

Leader: *If you're happy and you know it, jump up and down.*

Movement: Jump four times.

Parting

Play the "Goodbye Song." Form a circle, holding hands, sway side to side, and wave good-bye.

Tiny Seeds

Tiny seeds all curled up tight

Sound asleep; it's night, night

Rain splashes all around

The sun comes up and warms
the ground

Tiny seeds shoot out your roots

A lovely tree, for all to see

From *Stories on the Move: Integrating Literature and Movement with Children, Infants to Age 14* by Arlene Cohen. Illustrated by Andrea Fitcha McAllister. Westport, CT: Libraries Unlimited. Copyright © 2007.

Planting a Sunflower Seed

Today, let's plant a sunflower

We know just how to cover the seed
most carefully

We know just how to cover the seed
most carefully

It's only a baby now

Each day it will grow and grow

For all to see

It's Raining; It's Pouring

It's raining, it's pouring;

The old man is snoring.

He bumped his head

And went to bed

*And couldn't get up in
the morning.*

Rain, rain, go away;

Come again another day;

We want to go out and play.

Harvest Hoedown

We have gathered our beautiful sunflowers. I'm very happy; are you? If you're happy and you know it, clap your hands.

If you're happy and your know it, clap your hands.

If you're happy and you know it, then your face will surely show it.

If you're happy and you know it, clap your hands.

If you're happy and you know it, stomp your feet.

If you're happy and you know it, stomp your feet.

If you're happy and you know it, then your face will surely show it.

If you're happy and you know it, stomp your feet.

If you're happy and you know it, jump up and down.

If you're happy and you know it, jump up and down.

If you're happy and you know it, then your face will surely show it.

If you're happy and you know it, jump up and down.

Program 2: Down on the Farm

Summary

Children enjoy a lively train ride to Old MacDonald's farm, visiting Mary and her garden on the way. "Tick Tock Time" keeps the program moving through rhyme, stories, songs, and rhythmic dances. Movement improvisations emphasize the use of large muscle groups, with dancing verbs and prepositions. Clapping syllables and rhymes also builds phonological awareness, the ability to hear and manipulate the smaller sounds in words. New words are learned as well. The program closes with a few questions about what the children did today. This program takes between 45 and 60 minutes.

Program Preparation

Books

Hickory, Dickory, Dock Books

- Chapman, Jane. *Sing a Song of Sixpence*: *A Pocketful of Nursery Rhymes and Tales*. Cambridge, MA: Candlewick Press, 2004.

- Marshall, James. *Hickory, Dickory, Dock: And Other Mother Goose Rhymes.* New York: Farrar, Straus & Giroux, 2003.

Train Books

- *Go, Train, Go!: A Thomas the Tank Engine Story.* Illustrated by Tommy Stubbs. New York: Random House, 2006. Easy-to-read, lyrical text tells how cautious Thomas gives a ride to a judge, who is in a big hurry to get to a train show.

- Mayo, Margaret. *Choo Choo Clickety-Clack!* Illustrated by Alex Ayliffe. Minneapolis, MN: Carolrhoda Books, 2005. Rhythmic sounds imitate trains, planes, and other busy means of transportation that come and go.

- Piper, Watty. *The Little Engine That Could.* New York: Philomel Books, in Association with Grosset and Dunlap, 2005. Although she is not very big, the Little Blue Engine agrees to try to pull a stranded train full of toys over the mountain.

Farm Books

- Dann, Penny. *Old Macdonald Had a Farm.* Hauppauge, NY: Barron's Educational Series, 1999.

- Kutner, Merrily. *Down on the Farm.* New York: Holiday House, 2004. Simple rhyming text describes the sounds and activities of animals during a day on the farm.

- McFarlane, Sheryl. *What's That Sound? On the Farm.* Illustrated by Kim LaFave. Allston, MA: Fitzhenry & Whiteside, 2003. How the animals sound and move, in rhyme.
- Weber, Vicky. *Animal Babies on the Farm.* Boston: Houghton Mifflin, 2005.
- Wells, Rosemary. *Old MacDonald.* New York: Scholastic, 1998.

Music

- Zydeco, Buckwheat. "Get on Board Little Children" song, from *Choo Choo Boogaloo.* Redway, CA: Music for Little People, 1994.

Music from Louisiana

- Giuliano, Christine. The "Tick-Tock" song, from *Spiritual Lullabies: Songs to Honor the Child Within.* Manhattan Beach, CA: Christine Abella Music, 2003.

Space Needs

- On one side of the room, have chairs set up in rows of two, to resemble seating on one side of a train, for the "Boogaloo Train Ride."
- Carpeted or smooth movement space, about 20 feet by 20 feet, for 10 toddlers and adults. Have one chair facing the front of the train chairs.

Materials and Equipment

- CD and cassette player
- Whiskers, or place your index finger parallel to and between your nose and lips to suggest whiskers, for the mouse in "Hickory Dickory Dock"
- Party horns for "Little Boy Blue"
- A real or toy large clock
- Handouts: rhymes included at end of this chapter (enlarge as needed)
- Two metal or plastic stands to hold enlarged rhymes

Before You Begin

- Gather or purchase and set up all materials and equipment.
- Make two enlarged copies of rhymes to display on stands on both sides of you for participants to say with you as you do the program.
- Read over and practice the words and movements in the program.

Program

Introduction

> Today's program is called "Down on the Farm." The clock will be ticking as we get ready for our trip, ride the train, and visit Old MacDonald. This program is an easy and fun way to introduce your toddler to literature and creative dance. The activities will pave the way for your child to read, listen, speak, and write, and to move gracefully. We are going to play *make believe;* we are going to take a make believe trip to a farm. Let's clap and say *make-be-lieve*. [Model clapping for the children and have them join you in clapping the three syllables three times.]

Story and Movement Time

Part 1: Starting Time (5–10 Minutes)

Leader: *What TIME is it?* [Move to in front of the children, pick up the clock, and look at the time.] *It's TIME to START!*

Up and Down and All Around (adapted from the traditional version)

1. Leader: *Which directions do my arms go? My arms go **up** and my arms go **down**.*

Movement: Stretch your arms over your head and then lower them back down to your sides.

2. Leader: *Which direction is my body going? My body turns **around** and **round**.*

Movement: Turn around in place a couple of times.

3. Leader: *Which direction do my legs go? My legs jump **up** and **down**.*

Movement: Jump and point up to the ceiling; when you land, press your palms toward the floor.

4. Leader: *Which direction do I sit? I sit **down**; and so do you.*

Movement: Keep pressing your palms toward the floor then and sit down.

5. Leader: *I can listen; I'll show you how.*

Movement: Cup the back of your ear and tilt it toward the children.

Leader: STORYTIME BEGINS RIGHT NOW!

Part 2: Tick Tock Time (15 Minutes)

Play the "Tick-Tock" song. Gather all the children into the movement space. Stand in the midst of the children. Move freely to the music and allow children to move spontaneously. This is unstructured movement. Move with a sense of freedom and the joy of starting a new day. Say the following verbs, common movements for this age, and do them as you say: *pulling, pushing, climbing, running,* and *jumping.* The children will either be doing similar movements or imitating you. Or, you might say and do the following:

> *I see you jump, and jump up, jump up, jump up*
>
> *I see you push and push out, push out, push out*
>
> *I see you pull, and pull in, pull in, pull in*
>
> *Fall down . . .*

Stop the music and ask the following:

Leader: *What TIME is it?* [Pick up the clock and look at the time.] *It's Tick Tock TIME!*

Read and show pictures from one of the "Hickory Dickory Dock" books. Stand in front of the children and perform the following for them. They will either imitate you or just dance around.

Hickory Dickory Dock (traditional rhyme)

1. Leader: *TICK TOCK TICK TOCK TICK TOCK Hickory Dickory*

Movement: Sway your body like a pendulum from side to side

I Am a Swinging Pendulum.

2. Leader: DOCK!

Movement: Lift up on the balls of your feet and sing "dock" in a high-pitched voice. Put on the whiskers, or put your finger below your nose, parallel to your lips.

3. Leader: *The little tiny mouse*

Can you be a little tiny mouse? Curl yourself up and make believe you're real small.

Movement: Everyone curls up on the floor, and then you get up quickly.

4. Leader: *Ran up the big clock. Can you make yourself real big?*

Movement: Uncurl yourself and extend your arms over your head, then lift up on the balls of your feet.

5. Leader: *The clock struck "1"*

Movement: Say "one" loudly and vibrate or shake your head.

6. Leader: *And down he ran that small little scared mouse. Can you make yourself real small?*

Movement: Lower your heels and bend your knees, then hide your face, curl yourself up, and look out from between your hands, side to side, making yourself really small, like a scared mouse.

7. Leader: *Hickory, Dickory, D-o-c-k. Now be a very big clock.*

Movement: Stand straight. Sway slowly from side to side. Say the word "Dock" slowly, in a low voice.

Repeat a second time. More children may imitate you the second time.

Part 3: Train Time (20 Minutes)

Read and show pictures from one of the train books. Have other train books for children to look at and turn the pages of.

Leader: *TICK TOCK TICK TOCK TICK TOCK*

Movement: Put the clock to your ear and listen to it as you speak.

Leader: *What time is it now? It's Boogaloo Train Ride Time. It's time to take a make-be-lieve* [clap with each syllable three times] *train to visit some friends down on the farm.*

[Play the beginning of the "Get on Board Little Children" song.]

Leader: *Let's hop on the Boogaloo Train.*

Movement: Have children sit in the train seats. Sit in a larger chair facing them. Bounce up and down in the chair, pulling imaginary chains with both hands, and repeat several times with the music.

Stop the music.

1. Leader: [Pointing out the imaginary train window, say] *there's Mary in her garden. She doesn't look very happy.*

Movement: Make a very sad face.

2. Leader: *Can you make a sad face?* [Give children a chance to make sad faces, keeping a pout on your face.]

Mary, Mary, Quite Extra Contrary (adapted from the traditional)

3. Leader: *Oh, Mary, Mary quite contrary*

Movement: Make more sad faces at everyone.

4. Leader: *What was Mary? con-trar-y*

Movement: Have them repeat the word "contrary" and clap three times for each syllable.

5. Leader: *She was very sad.*

Movement: Make sad faces.

6. Leader: *Really! How does your garden grow?*

Movement: Throw your arms up in the air, as if to say, "how in the world can such an unhappy person grow a garden?"

7. Leader: [Using Mary's voice, speak sweetly and sound a bit crazy.] *With cockleshells and silver bells.*

What did she say? Cockleshells and silver bells?" Really! Cockleshells and Silver Bells?!

[In Mary's voice, shout *YES!* (in a prissy voice).] *And all little maids in a row.*

What did she say? All little maids in a row! Really!

Mary's not very happy, is she? But I am; how about you?

Leader: *Let's go do a happy dance.*

Movement: Take the children off the train and back to the movement space.

If You're Happy and You Know It (traditional song)

1. Leader: *If you're happy and you know it, clap your hands.*

Movement: Clap your hands three times.

2. Leader: *If you're happy and you know it, clap you hands.*

Movement: Clap your hands three times.

3. Leader: *If you're happy and you know it, then your face will surely show it.*

Movement: Smile and point to your face.

4. Leader: *If you're happy and you know it, clap your hands.*

Movement: Clap your hands three times.

5. Leader: *If you're happy and you know it, stomp your feet.*

Movement: Stomp your feet three times.

6. Leader: *If you're happy and you know it, stomp your feet.*

Movement: Stomp your feet three times.

7. Leader: *If you're happy and you know it, then your face will surely show it.*

Movement: Smile and point to your face.

8. Leader: *If you're happy and you know it, stomp your feet.*

Movement: Stomp your feet three times.

Leader: *If you're happy and you know it, jump up and down.*

Movement: Jump four times.

Leader: *If you're happy and you know it, jump up and down.*

Movement: Jump four times.

Leader: *If you're happy and you know it, then your face will surely show it.*

Movement: Smile and point to your face.

Leader: *If you're happy and you know it, jump up and down.*

Movement: Jump four times.

Part 4: Farm Time (15 Minutes)

Leader: *Here we are at the farm.* [Read and show pictures in one of the farm books.]
   Let's do the Old MacDonald dance. [The children may imitate you or just do whatever they want as you sing or say the words.]

Old MacDonald (traditional rhyme)

   1. Leader: *Old MacDonald had a farm, E-I-E-I-O*

   Movement: On the E-I-E-I-O, open your arms away from your body, making a round shape that grows larger as you open your arms.

   2. Leader: *With a moo, moo here, to the left.*

   Movement: Walk diagonally to the left, saying "moo, moo."

   3. Leader: *And a moo, moo there, to the right.*

   Movement: Walk diagonally to the right.

4. Leader: *Here a moo, there a moo.*

Movement: Walk one step to the right, then one step to the left.

5. Leader: *Everywhere a moo, moo.*

Movement: Turn your body to the right, then to the left.

6. Leader: *Old MacDonald had a farm, E-I-E-I-O!*

Movement: On the E-I-E-I-O, open your arms away from your body, making a round shape that grows larger as you open your arms.

Little Boy Blue (adapted from the traditional version)

Leader: *Oh!* [Sound startled.] *The sheep's in the meadow. Baa! Baa!* [Have the children say "baa, baa."]

The cow's in the corn. Moo! Moo! [Have the children say "moo, moo."]

Little Boy Blue, come blow your horn. [Give the children party horns to blow.]

Where is the boy who looks after the sheep? Is he fast asleep? No? He's blowing his horn.

[Encourage the children to play horns for a while.]

Part 5: Train Time to Go Home (5 Minutes)

Leader: *Oh! TICK TOCK TICK TOCK TICK TOCK.* [Put the clock to your ear and listen to it as you speak.] *What time is it now? It's Boogaloo Train Ride Time. It's time to go home.* [Play the "Get on Board Little Children" song.]

Let's hop on the Boogaloo Train.

Movement: Have the children sit in the "train seats." Sit in a larger chair in front of them. Bounce up and down in the chair, pulling imaginary chains with both hands, and repeat several times.

Leader: *Did you have fun today? What did we do today?* [You may want to mention some of the events, characters, animals, etc., and see how they respond.]

Up and Down and All Around

Which directions do my arms go? My arms go up and my arms go down.

Which direction is my body going? My body turns around and round.

Which direction do my legs go? My legs jump up and down.

Which direction do I sit? I sit down; and so do you.

I can listen; I'll show you how.

Story time begins right now!

Mary, Mary, Quite Extra Contrary

Oh, Mary, Mary quite contrary

What was Mary? con-trar-y

She was very sad.

Really! How does your garden grow?

(Using Mary's voice, speak sweet and sound a bit crazy).

With cockleshells and silver bells

What did she say? Cockleshells and silver bells? Really! Cockleshells and Silver Bells?

(Mary shouts) *YES!* (Prissy) *And all little maids in a row.*

What did she say? All little maids in a row! Really!

Little Boy Blue

Oh! The sheep's in the meadow.

Baa! Baa!

The cow's in the corn.

Moo! Moo!

Little Boy Blue, come blow your horn.
Where is the Boy who looks after the
sheep? Is he fast asleep?
No? He's blowing his horn.

Chapter 3

Dance-About Programs for Preschoolers: Ages Three to Five

Introduction

The "Dance-About" programs engage the child in co-creating story narrative and improvising movement based on literary imagery. Rhythmic and fun or humorous poems, songs, and stories serve as a catalyst for literacy development and movement improvisations. The themes help children explore and learn how the world works beyond the home. Singing games, familiar to many generations, round out the programs. Activities are designed to promote early literacy as they simultaneously refine mind-body coordination, expand vocabulary, and build grammatical skills. A preschool age child is very active and speaks in whole sentences. Dancing verbs and prepositions are enhanced by dancing adjectives and adverbs, as the child surges high in the air, turns around, pushes gently, and pulls slowly in response to the literary imagery. If the leader of the program does not have a background in storytelling and wishes to perform the literature, see the handout "Trigger Method of Learning a Story (Group Leader)" at the end of chapter 6.

As the preschooler interacts in the program activities, he or she is encouraged to ask questions and tell about what has happened in the story. These programs encourage language development and problem solving by using the imagination in role-playing story characters and creating story solutions. Early literacy skills are built through dialoging with the reader, being read to, having objects pointed out in the books, hearing new words, and responding to "open-ended questions" during reading. The child becomes aware of how words flow on the page from top-to-bottom and left-to-right. If the story, poem, or rhyme is told rather than read, the child learns that a story is a way of communicating orally. Children clap out syllables, learn the alphabet, and practice writing on paper and in the air.

The combination of movement and literature develops the abundance of neural connections in the preschooler's brain. The repetition of sounds and movement and a variety of vocal intonations and rhythms encourage the language, listening, observation, imaginative, and movement skills of the child. Details about preschoolers' cognitive, physical, and emergent literacy skills are outlined in Table 3.1.

Table 3.1. Readiness to Learn (Preschoolers)

COGNITIVE	PHYSICAL	LITERACY BUILDING
<ul><li>Is talkative; uses many new words, sentences</li><li>Uses egocentric speech</li><li>Believes in magic</li><li>Has perceptions dominating judgment</li><li>Recognizes problems and works on solving them</li><li>Asks and answers many questions</li><li>Understands daily routines, seasons</li><li>Uses counting, alphabet, size relationships, colors</li><li>Is aware of feelings and feeling words</li><li>Likes to put on dress-up clothes</li><li>Likes a good story picture book and questions about the story, music, rhymes, poetry, nonfiction</li><li>Begins to imagine and think symbolically</li><li>Likes to role play and make up stories</li><li>Can describe what is seen and felt</li><li>Lives in the present moment</li></ul>	<ul><li>Exhibits beginning of symbolic play</li><li>Has more refined use of muscles and motor skills</li><li>Improvises movement</li><li>Has spatial orientation</li><li>Can turn, swing, and rock</li><li>Can move in a circle formation</li><li>Can imitate movement of leader for singing games</li><li>Can move in a specified direction</li><li>Can use body to make shapes and change the size of the shape</li><li>Can change the quality of the movement, like moving quickly or slowly.</li></ul>	*Reading awareness:* <ul><li>Understands flow of words from top-to-bottom, left-to-right</li><li>Understands print being read by someone</li><li>Points to words on page as reader says them</li><li>Reads signs, labels, lists, menus, etc.</li></ul>*Engaging in book sharing:* <ul><li>"Reads" story from memory</li><li>Likes to go to library and bookstores</li><li>Reads same stories many times</li><li>Should be surrounded with books</li></ul>*Awareness of letters:* <ul><li>Caregiver should write words that interest the child.</li><li>In alphabet books the child can point to and name letters.</li></ul>*Learning new words/conversing:* <ul><li>Point to pictures to have child identify new words.</li><li>Ask "what" questions related to characters, setting, and plot. Brainstorm about the plot of the story.</li><li>Add to the child's responses to the reading.</li><li>Read books on topics that interest the child.</li><li>Talk about how things work, feelings, and ideas.</li></ul>*Speaking and thinking skills:* <ul><li>Understands and tell stories</li><li>Describes things, events; asks open-ended questions</li><li>Can relate story events to own experience</li></ul>

COGNITIVE	PHYSICAL	LITERACY BUILDING
		Awareness of letters and word formations:
		➢ Understands that letters have names and sounds
		➢ Begins to write name, familiar words
		Literary resources:
		➢ Books that tell stories that make children laugh
		➢ Simple text
		➢ Things about other kids, going to school, friends
		➢ Playful or rhyming, alphabet, counting
		Syllable awareness:
		➢ Hears and manipulates the smaller sounds in words
		➢ Can hear and create rhymes
		➢ Can combine syllables
		➢ Fills in the words in repetitive books
		➢ Claps out syllables of own name
		➢ Reads stories and poems that rhyme

These programs are thematic to engage parents or caregivers, which in turn will engage children. Small children learn from and enjoy watching, listening to, and imitating what their significant adults do and say. Everyone can dance in the "Dance-About" programs: children and adults!

Program 1: Why, Oh, Why?

Summary

Questions! Questions! Questions! Have fun answering: **Why** did the old woman swallow the fly? **Where** did that gingerbread boy go? **What's** on Fred's head? **How** do you go Lobby Loo? **When** are we going to go home? Improvisational and guided movement and conversations will "wriggle and jiggle and tickle" the children, as they propose their own answers to life's quandaries, real and imagined. The "Wheels on the Bus" song winds them to and from story time, and they go goodbye with "A Bushel and a Peck." This program lasts about one hour.

Program Preparation

Books

- Egielski, Richard. *The Gingerbread Boy.* New York: HarperCollins, 1997; or
- Galdone, Paul. *The Gingerbread Boy.* New York: Seabury Press [1975].
- *There Was an Old Woman Who Swallowed a Fly.* Text is included in this program.

Poems

- Prelutsky, Jack. "As Soon as Fred Gets out of Bed." In *Something BIG Has Been Here.* New York: Greenwillow, 1990.
- Prelutsky, Jack, comp. "Be Glad Your Nose Is on Your Face." In *For Laughing Out Loud: Poems to Tickle Your Funnybone.* Illustrated by Marjorie Priceman. New York: Knopf, distributed by Random House, 1991.

Music

- Gallina, Jill. "Shoo Fly, Don't Bother Me" song, from *Hand Jivin'.* Freeport, NY: Educational Activities, 1996.
- "Looby Loo" and "A Bushel and a Peck" songs, from *Four Baby Bumblebees.* Long Branch, NJ: Kimbo Educational, 2001.
- "Wheels on the Bus" song, from *Mommy & Me: Playgroup Favorites.* Beverly Hills, CA: Concord, 2004.

Space Needs

- About 2 square feet of open space for each child, carpeted or hard floor with cushions.

Equipment and Materials

- CD and cassette player
- A pair of little boy's underwear

Before You Begin

- Gather equipment and materials.
- Review and practice the program.

Program

Introduction

> Our program today is called "Why Oh Why"; it's about asking questions and answering them in a fun way. [Ask the children:] Do you ever ask questions? You learn a lot when you ask questions, don't you? What questions do you ask? [Give them some time to brainstorm about questions they ask.] Some questions begin with "why," some begin with "where," some begin with "what," some begin with "how," and some begin with "when." Our stories, songs, and dances today will help us answer why, where, what, how, and when!

Story and Movement Time (10 Minutes)

Part 1: Bus Ride (5 Minutes)

Leader: *Let's take the bus to story time.* [Play "Wheels on the Bus."]

Let the children warm up by dancing freely around the room; they will be motivated by the music and your free-form movement. Dancing with them and having fun copying their unique movements will develop rapport with them and build their self-esteem.

Part 2: Hands Go Up, Hands Go Down (5 Minutes)

Say or sing this traditional rhyme to the children, to the tune of "Twinkle, Twinkle, Little Star."

1. Leader: *Hands go up and hands go down.*

Movement: Reach up over your head and then drop your arms.

2. Leader: *I can turn around and round.*

Movement: Turn around in place.

3. Leader: *I can hop upon one shoe.*

Movement: Hop on one foot.

4. Leader: *I can sit and so can you.*

Movement: Sit down and press your palms in the direction of the floor to signal that you want the children to sit down.

5. Leader: *I can listen, I'll show you how.*

Movement: Soften your voice and cup your ear.

6. Leader: *Story Time begins right now.*

Part 3: "Why" Questions (10 Minutes)

Leader: *Sometimes we ask questions that begin with "why," like: "Why did that happen?" or "Why do I have to brush my teeth again?" or "Why do I have to go to bed now?" or "Why does the elephant have such a long nose and such a short tail?" or "Why is the giraffe's neck so long?" Well, I'm sure we all want to know why, oh, why an old woman swallowed a fly.*

Read or tell *There Was an Old Woman Who Swallowed a Fly.* Sit in a chair, but stand up and wriggle and jiggle for the following line in each stanza: "That wriggled and jiggled and tickled inside her." Have the children stand up quickly and join you for the movement and then sit down again quickly, each time you say the line.

There Was an Old Woman (traditional story)

> **Leader:** *There was an old woman who swallowed a fly,*
>
> *I don't know why she swallowed a fly,*
>
> *Perhaps she'll die.*
>
>
> *There was an old woman who swallowed a spider,*
>
> ***That wriggled and jiggled and tickled inside her,***
>
> *She swallowed the spider to catch the fly,*
>
> *I don't know why she swallowed the fly,*
>
> *Perhaps she'll die.*
>
>
> *There was an old woman who swallowed a bird,*
>
> *How absurd! to swallow a bird,*
>
> *She swallowed the bird to catch the spider,*
>
> ***That wriggled and jiggled and tickled inside her,***
>
> *She swallowed the spider to catch the fly,*
>
> *I don't know why she swallowed the fly,*
>
> *Perhaps she'll die.*
>
>
> *There was an old woman, who swallowed a cat,*
>
> *Imagine that! to swallow a cat, MEOW!*
>
> *She swallowed the cat to catch the bird,*
>
> *She swallowed the bird to catch the spider,*
>
> ***That wriggled and jiggled and tickled inside her,***

She swallowed the spider to catch the fly,

I don't know why she swallowed the fly,

Perhaps she'll die.

There was an old woman who swallowed a dog,

What a hog! to swallow a dog, BOW WOW!

She swallowed the dog to catch the cat,

She swallowed the cat to catch the bird,

She swallowed the bird to catch the spider,

That wriggled and jiggled and tickled inside her,

She swallowed the spider to catch the fly,

I don't know why she swallowed the fly,

Perhaps she'll die.

There was an old woman who swallowed a goat,

Just opened her throat! to swallow a goat, NEE, NEE!

She swallowed the goat to catch the dog,

She swallowed the dog to catch the cat,

She swallowed the cat to catch the bird,

She swallowed the bird to catch the spider,

That wriggled and jiggled and tickled inside her,

She swallowed the spider to catch the fly,

I don't know why she swallowed the fly,

Perhaps she'll die.

There was an old woman who swallowed a cow,

I don't know how she swallowed a cow! MOO-UU!

She swallowed the cow to catch the goat,

She swallowed the goat to catch the dog,

She swallowed the dog to catch the cat,

She swallowed the cat to catch the bird,

She swallowed the bird to catch the spider,

That wriggled and jiggled and tickled inside her,

She swallowed the spider to catch the fly,

I don't know why she swallowed the fly.

So, if a fly came by you, what would you do? Would you swallow it? [Give them a chance to make up something.]
I would say to the fly: "Shoo fly, don't bother me!

Part 4: Shoo Fly (5 Minutes)

Play "Shoo Fly, Don't Bother Me" from *Hand Jivin'*. Do the following movements for the children to imitate.

Shoo Fly (traditional song)

1. Leader: *Help me swat this fly.*

Shoo, fly, don't bother me,

Movement: Wave your hand and arm as if to swat a fly in front of you.

2. Leader: *Shoo, fly, don't bother me,*

Movement: Wave your right arm and hand as if to swat a fly to your right side.

3. Leader: *Shoo, fly, don't bother me,*

Movement: Wave your left arm and hand as if to swat a fly to your left side.

4. Leader: *For I belong to somebody.*

Movement: Spin around in place and clap your hands.

5. Leader: *I feel, I feel*

Movement: Tap your chest twice, then rotate your upper body to the right and the left.

6. Leader: *I feel like a morning star,*

Movement: With your arms raised diagonally toward the ceiling, sway to the right and the left.

7. Leader: *I feel, I feel,*

Movement: Tap your chest twice, then rotate your upper body to the right and the left

8. Leader: *I feel like a morning star.*

Movement: With your arms raised diagonally toward the ceiling, sway to the right and the left.

Repeat the song and all movements.

Part 5: "Where" Questions (10 Minutes)

Ask the children to sit down.

Leader: *Sometimes we ask questions that begin with "where," like, "Where are we going?" or "Where is my mommy?" Well, I'm sure we all want to know where, oh where, did that gingerbread boy go? You are going to be gingerbread people in just a few minutes.* [Seat all children on one side of the movement space. Divide children into groups of four. Give each group a number; one group at a time will be the gingerbread boy on the run. Have each group repeat their number a few times, as you point to that group.]

Remember now, do not run until I point to your group and say your number. [The refrain is repeated four times. They will run from one side of the room to the other.]

Read or tell one of the Gingerbread Boy books. Call the number of each group and have the group children stand up and run across the room when you read the refrain,

Leader: *Run, run, as fast as you can, you can't catch me, I'm the gingerbread man!* [Encourage all children to repeat the refrain with you.]

Part 6: What Questions (5—10 Minutes)

Leader: *Sometimes we ask questions that begin with "what," like: "What time is it?" Or "What's your name?" Well, I'm sure we all want to know what, oh what is on Fred's head?*

Read or recite the poem, "As Soon as Fred Gets out of Bed." Put the little boy's underwear on your head when Fred does it in the poem.

Leader: *What did Fred put on his head? Why did he do that?* [Give the children time to answer.] *Is there a nose on the top of my head?* [Give them a chance to respond.]

Read or recite "Be Glad your Nose Is on Your Face."

Part 7: "How" Questions (10 Minutes)

Leader: *Sometimes we ask questions that begin with "how," like: "How are you today"? or "How did you do that?" Well, I'm sure we all want to know how, oh how we go Lobby Loo.* [Play the "Looby Loo" song . Have children hold hands and form a circle.]

Looby Loo (traditional song)

1. Leader: *Now we dance looby loo,*

Now we dance looby light,

Now we dance looby loo,

Movement: Hold hands and move counterclockwise in the circle.

2. Leader: *All on a Saturday night*

Movement: Stop and clap your hands on the word "night."

3. Leader: *You put your right hand in*

Movement: Turn the right side of your body toward the center of the circle and put your right hand and arm inside the circle.

4. Leader: *You take your right hand out*

Movement: Turn the right side of your body toward the outside of the circle and put your right hand and arm outside the circle.

5. Leader: *You give your hand a shake, shake, shake*

Movement: Face the center of the circle and shake your right arm and hand.

6. Leader: *And turn yourself about*

Movement: Spin to the right in place.

7. Leader: *Here we go looby loo; Here we go looby light; Here we go looby loo*

Movement: Hold hands and move clockwise in the circle.

8. Leader: *All on a Saturday night*

Movement: Clap your hands on the word "night."

9. Leader: *You put your left hand in*

Movement: Turn the left side of your body toward the center of the circle and put your left hand and arm inside the circle.

10. Leader: *You take your left hand out*

Movement: Turn the left side of your body toward the outside of the circle and put your left hand and arm outside the circle.

11. Leader: *You give your hand a shake, shake, shake*

Movement: Face the center of the circle and shake your left arm and hand.

12. Leader: *And turn yourself about*

Movement: Spin to the left in place.

13. Leader: *Here we go looby loo; Here we go looby light; Here we go looby loo*

Movement: Hold hands and move counterclockwise in the circle.

14. Leader: *All on a Saturday night*

Movement: Clap your hands on the word "night."

15. Leader: *You put your right foot in*

Movement: Turn the right side of your body toward the center of the circle and put your right foot and leg inside the circle.

16. Leader: *You take your right foot out*

Movement: Turn the right side of your body toward the outside of the circle and put your right foot and leg outside the circle.

17. Leader: *You give your right foot a shake, shake*

Movement: Face the center of the circle and shake your right arm and hand.

18. Leader: *And turn yourself about*

Movement: Spin to the right in place.

19. Leader: *Here we go looby loo; Here we go looby light; Here we go looby loo*

Movement: Hold hands and move clockwise in the circle.

20. Leader: *All on a Saturday night*

Movement: Clap your hands on the word "night."

21. Leader: *You put your left foot in*

Movement: Turn the left side of your body toward the center of the circle and put your left foot and leg inside the circle.

22. Leader: *You take your left foot out*

Movement: Turn the left side of your body toward the outside of the circle and put your left foot and leg outside the circle.

23. Leader: *You give your foot a shake, shake, shake*

Movement: Face the center of the circle and shake your left foot and leg.

24. Leader: *And turn yourself about*

Movement: Spin to the left in place.

25. Leader: *Here we go looby loo. Here we go looby light. Here we go looby loo.*

Movement: Hold hands and move counterclockwise in the circle.

26. Leader: *All on a Saturday night*

Movement: Clap your hands on the word "night."

27. Leader: *You put your whole self in*

Movement: Jump into the circle.

28. Leader: *You take your whole self out*

29. Movement: Jump backwards.

30. Leader: *You give your whole self a shake, shake, shake*

Movement: Shake from head to toe.

31. Leader: *And turn yourself about*

Movement: Turn around to the right and then to the left. **CLAP HANDS!!**

Part 8: "When" Questions (5—10 Minutes)

Leader: *Sometimes we ask questions that begin with "when," like "When, oh, when will the bus come, so we can go home?"*

Play "Wheels on the Bus" and again let the children dance freely, dancing with them.

Play "A Bushel and a Peck." Everybody gives everybody else a goodbye hug and a peck (kiss) on the cheek.

Program 2: Let's Go to the Circus!

Summary

Children dance in the Circus Bus on the way to and from the Big Top. Under the Big Top, the circus master introduces the famous performer, Eleanor the elephant. They learn what an "encore" means and create an encore for Eleanor. When the circus master introduces the trapeze artists, the children improvise a swinging, name-writing-flying dance. They dance to and learn adverbial phrases. The children then watch as Myrtle the clown does her girdle act. Clowning around continues with clothes from the dress-up box in the "Clowning Around" dance. This program takes between 45 minutes and an hour.

Program Preparation

Books

- Peet, William B. *Encore for Eleanor*. Boston: Houghton Mifflin, 1981 and 1985. Eleanor the elephant, a retired circus star, finds a new career as the resident artist in the city zoo.

Alternative Circus Stories and Poems

- Falk, Barbara *Bustetter*. [New York]: HarperCollins, 1993. After being captured for a Russian circus, Grusha the bear learns his tricks well, but despite his new-found fame, he longs to return to the forest.

- Freeman, Don. *Bearymore*. New York: Viking Press, 1976. A circus bear has trouble hibernating and dreaming up a new act at the same time.

- Hopkins, Lee Bennett, comp. *Circus! Circus!: Poems*. Illustrated by John O'Brien. New York: Knopf, distributed by Random House, 1982.

- Murphy, Stuart J. *Circus Shapes*. Illustrated by Edward Miller. New York: HarperCollins, 1998. Circus animals and performers getting ready for a show form basic geometric shapes.

- Prelutsky, Jack. *Circus*. Illustrated by Arnold Lobel. New York: Macmillan, [1974].

Music

- Arnold, Linda. "Circus Train," "Midway," "Crazy Clowns," "Under the Big Top," and "King of the Flying Trapeze," from *Circus Magic: Under the Big Top*. Cypress, CA: Ariel Records, distributed by Youngheart Music, 1998.

- "Goodbye Song," from *Mommy & Me: Playgroup Favorites*. Beverly Hills, CA: Concord, 2004.

- "Man on the Flying Trapeze," from *101 Favorite Children's Songs*. Vol. 2, H-R. Hauppauge, NY: SPJ Music, 1999.

Space Needs

- Approximately 2 square feet for each child to move in, carpeted or hard floor.

Materials and Equipment

- CD and cassette player
- Poster board with the word "Encore" written on it
- Box of dress-up clothes and hats for clown dance
- Waist-type girdle for clown poem
- Blond wig and sunglasses for clown poem
- Gray felt or poster paper and scissors to make elephant ears
- Stretchable head band on which to attach elephant ears
- Two medium-sized safety pins to pin elephant ears to head band
- Circus master costume: top hat, bow tie, coat with tails or sport coat (coat optional)

Before You Begin

- Gather the box of clothing and costumes.
- Make the elephant ears (template in Figure 3.1).
- Review and practice the program.

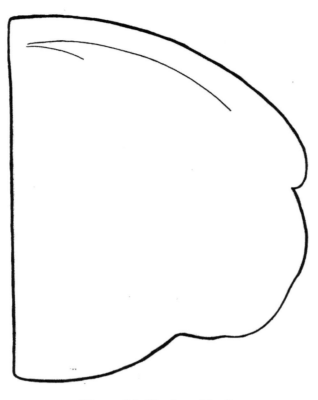

Figure 3.1. Elephant Ear Pattern.

Program

Introduction

Let's go to the circus today, where we will see Eleanor the dancing elephant, the trapeze artists, and the clowns. But first we must learn a new word: "Encore." [Show the word on the poster board and define it.] *Encore* means a demand by an audience for an additional performance, usually expressed by applause. Can you applaud loudly? Can you applaud softly? Can you applaud and yell out "encore," "encore for Eleanor"? We will do that again when Eleanor does her act.

Story and Movement Time

Part 1: Circus Train (5 Minutes)

Leader: *Here comes the Circus Train; let's hop on board.* [Play "Circus Train." Children improvise movement, free form.] *We've arrived at the circus; everybody find a seat; the show is going to start.* [Play "Midway."]

Part 2: Encore for Eleanor (15 Minutes)

Leader as Circus Master: [Put on your top hat and bow tie.] *Welcome one, welcome all to the greatest show on Earth. May I introduce the one, the only, stilt-dancing elephant; let's hear it for Eleanor, the famous elephant. Clap and yell "Encore for Eleanor," yeah!* [Costume change: Put on grey felt elephant ears.]

Read or tell *Encore for Eleanor.*

Leader: *What else could Eleanor have done for an encore?* [Give them a chance to make up something fantastic.] *Maybe she could have learned how to fly through the air???*

Part 3: Trapeze Artists (10 Minutes)

Change into the circus master costume. Play "King of the Flying Trapeze" or "Man on the Flying Trapeze."

Leader: *And now we have the trapeze artists performing.* [Invite the children into the movement space and have them pretend that they are flying through the air, swinging about the clouds, catching a star, and writing their names or the first letter of their names in the air, as they fly about.]

Part 4: Clowning Around (15 Minutes)

Leader as Circus Master: *And now may I introduce Myrtle, the clown?* [Dress yourself up in some crazy-looking outfit, with a girdle, a blonde wig, and sunglasses from the dress-up box, and recite or read the following clown poem.]

Myrtle's Girdle (original poem)

> *I won't jump over a hurdle, oh no*
>
> *because I'm wearing my new magnificent girdle.*
>
> *It's not just any girdle, you see;*
>
> *It belonged to the famous She,*
>
> *Miss Marilyn Monroe*
>
> *A Hollywood movie star, of long, long ago*
>
> *So, when you see me*
>
> *You'll know,*
>
> *I'll not be jumping to and fro*
>
> *I'll be looking good*
>
> *Standing, right where I stood*
>
> [Play "Crazy Clowns" and "Under the Big Top."]

The children select and put on clothes and hats from the dress-up box. Form a circle. The children should turn counterclockwise and move forward in that direction, making up a shaking-and-moving dance around the circle. Have the children turn toward the center. One by one, each child should go to the center of the circle and lead a "very silly movement" for those in the circle to follow. They may also add dialogue or sounds, if they wish.

Part 5: Circus Train Home (5 Minutes)

Leader: *Oh, here comes our bus; it's time to go home.* [Play "Circus Train" and let the children dance freely. Then play "Goodbye Song." Everybody holds hands in a circle and waves good-bye to each other.]

Program 3: Ocean's Alive!—Snorkeling and Diving with the Dolphins

Summary

Children explore reefs by browsing books on reefs and the marine animals that live there. After making snorkel masks, the children dance a "swim" out to a coral reef. On the way back they are greeted by a pod of bottlenose dolphins. They hear a story about dolphins, look at books about dolphins, and dance a "swim" with the dolphins. Literacy is reinforced by dancing prepositions and adverbs. This program is approximately one hour long.

Program Preparation

Books

Reef Books

- Pallotta, Jerry. *The Underwater Alphabet Book.* Illustrated by Edgar Stewart. Watertown, MA: Charlesbridge, 1991. Introduces the letters A to Z to describe fish and other creatures living in the coral reef.

Reef Books for Children to Browse

- Cerullo, Mary M. *Coral Reef: A City That Never Sleeps.* Photographs by Jeffrey L. Rotman. New York: Cobblehill Books, 1996.
- Fleisher, Paul. *Coral Reef.* New York: Benchmark Books/Marshall Cavendish, 1998.
- Pringle, Laurence. *Coral Reefs: Earth's Undersea Treasures.* New York: Simon & Schuster Books for Young Readers, 1995.
- Taylor, Barbara. *Coral Reef.* Photographs by Jane Burton. New York: Dorling Kindersley, 1992.

Dolphin Books

- Pfeiffer, Wendy. *Dolphin Talk: Whistles, Clicks, and Clapping Jaws.* Illustrated by Helen K. Davie. New York: HarperCollins, 2003.

Dolphin Books for Children to Browse

- Grooms, Molly, and Takashi Oda. *We Are Dolphins*. Minnetonka, MN: NorthWord Press, 2002. The story of a dolphin's first few days of life.
- Harris, Caroline. *Whales and Dolphins*. Boston: Kingfisher, 2005.
- Miller-Schroeder, Patricia. *Bottlenose Dolphins*. Austin, TX: Raintree Steck-Vaughn Publishers, 2002.

Music

- "Malibu Surf" and ocean sounds, from *Hush Little Baby: Soothing Sounds for Sleep*. Pacific Palisades, CA: Kids Music Factory, 2003.
- "Strange Creatures on the Reef," "Whale and Dolphin Sounds," and "The Coral Reef," from *Rock 'n Learn Oceans*. Conroe, Texas: Rock 'N Learn, 1998.

Space Needs

- Approximately 2 square feet for each child to move in, carpeted or hard floor.

Material and Equipment

- CD and cassette player
- Tables and chairs that can be easily moved to the sides, if space is limited
- Heavyweight (24 lb.) 8½-by-11-inch copy paper, one-half sheet for each child
- Crayons and preschool scissors for each child
- One or more single hole punches to make holes for string
- Hole reinforcements, four for each mask
- String to tie masks on (18 inches for each mask), cut in half
- Flex straws, one for each child
- Doublestick tape or glue to adhere straw onto mask
- About 30 inches of brightly colored 1-inch adhesive tape to mark the setting on the floor
- Blackboard or two pieces of poster paper, and chalk or marker for new words: *surge* and *profusely*
- Chart of alphabet letters

Before You Begin

- Gather the craft materials at the tables.
- Mark the setting (shore, reef, large rock) on the floor with the brightly colored tape.
- Copy the snorkel mask pattern on paper (template and instructions in Figure 3.2) for each child.
- Make up a snorkel mask and tube (straw) as a sample for the children.
- Review and practice the program.

1. Cut along the dotted lines.

2. Punch holes in the small circles and paste on hole reinforcements on both sides of the paper.

3. Cut the 18-inch string into two pieces and tie each one onto a hole.

4. Glue or tape a flex straw to the right side of mask to serve as the snorkel.

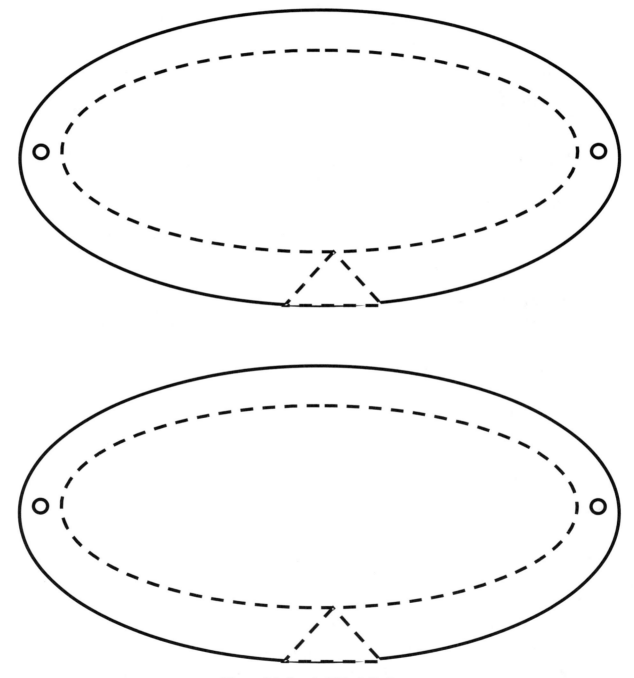

Figure 3.2. Snorkel Mask Pattern.

Program

Introduction

> [Play "Malibu Surf" as background music.] Our program today is called "Ocean's Alive." We are going snorkeling around the reef and diving with the dolphins. [Hold up words written on poster paper or write new words on the board.] Here are some new words. The first one is "surge." *Surge* is a smooth and quick way of jumping. It means to rise up smoothly and quickly, high up into the air. Dolphins don't just jump, they surge into the air. We will be doing that later. The other word is "profusely," which means doing something in a big way, with a lot of action. Dolphins shake themselves off profusely. We will do that in a while too! Before we read an alphabet book about animals that live on or near the coral reefs, we need to brush up on our letters of the alphabet. [Show and review chart of alphabet letters.]

Story and Movement Time

Part 1: Snorkling on the Coral Reefs (30 Minutes with Craft)

Read the introduction and the entries for letters A–D in *The Underwater Alphabet Book.* Show pictures and have children browse the books about coral reefs. Point out how the words go from top to bottom and side to side on the page.

Leader: *Before we go for a swim out to the coral reefs, let's make some snorkel masks!*

Story Craft: Snorkel Mask

Have the children color and cut out the snorkel mask pattern. They should wear the snorkeling gear so they can dive into the song imagery. Take children to the setting area marked on the floor.

Snorkeling

Prepositions to emphasize are in boldface type.

1. Leader: *Show me how you swim. Let's swim **around** the whole ocean. Say "swimming **around and around and around**."*

2. Leader: *Let's swim **between** the big rock and the coral reef; make yourself very narrow. Say "swimming **between and between and between**."*

3. Leader: *Let's swim **towards** the other end of the reef. Say "swimming **towards and towards and towards**."*

4. Leader: *Let's swim **backwards**, away from the reef. Say "swimming **backwards and backwards and backwards**."*

5. Leader: *Let's swim **over** and **under** the reef. Say "swimming **over** and **under, over** and **under**, and **over** and **under**."*

Play "Coral Reef" or "Strange Creatures on the Reef" (rap). Encourage children to continue swimming in different directions during the music by calling out "swim around," "swim between," "swim toward," "swim backward," "swim over," and "swim under," and by using any other prepositions that seem appropriate with the song. The children may spontaneously become the sea animals as they are described in the song, but they can also react to them spatially with the prepositions as you call them out, for example, "swim around the turtle" or "swim toward the starfish."

Part 2: Diving with the Dolphins (20 Minutes)

Have children look at books on dolphins and show the covers. Read *Dolphin Talk: Whistles, Clicks, and Clapping Jaws.* Practice dolphin talk with children, varying the tones.

Focus

Adverbs to emphasize are in boldface type.

1. Leader: *Now we are going to practice our dolphin movements. You are a dolphin, surging **lightly** out of the water, up into the air; you dive **sharply** back into the water. Say surging **lightly**, diving **sharply** as you do those movements. When you jump and land, do both with bent knees.*

Movement: Bend your knees, stretch your arms overhead, and jump lightly up into the air, landing on bent knees. Arch your back and curve your arms slightly forward from the overhead stretched position. Point your fingers down sharply and bend toward the floor.

I Am a Dolphin.

2. Leader: *Repeat number 1 several times*

3. Leader: *Bring your head out of the water, making dolphin sounds., Clap your jaws and smile **brightly**. Say "smiling **brightly**" just before you make your big dolphin smile.*

Movement: Stretch your neck out long, make dolphin sounds, clap your jaws, and make a huge smile.

4. Leader: *The dolphins are getting ready to swim off now and are saying good-bye in a show-off way. Say "shaking **profusely** and diving **sharply**" as you do these movements.*

Movement: Wiggle or shake profusely and dive sharply back into the water and away, whistling or clicking good-bye, and waving an arm quickly behind you like a fin in motion

Play "Whale and Dolphin Sounds." Encourage children to do the movement that you just practiced: to stretch and surge or jump up lightly, dive sharply, wiggle and shake profusely, wave quickly, and talk like a dolphin to the music.

Program 4: Ocean's Alive!—Submarine Trip

Summary

After the children hear a story about a submarine, they dance their way into the "Yellow Submarine" for an adventure under the sea. They hear a story about marine animals and do marine animal dances. They hear another story about an octopus and do a dance in the "Octopus's Garden." They learn adverbial phrases by saying them as they dance them. This program is approximately one hour long.

Program Preparation

Books

Submarine Books

• Ashman, Linda. *Rub-a-Dub Sub*. Illustrated by Jeff Mack. San Diego: Harcourt, 2003. A young boy meets many friendly sea animals as he travels underwater in his bright orange submarine

Submarine Books for Children to Browse

• Kramer, S. A. *Submarines*. New York: Random House, 2005.

• Mallard, Neil, in association with The U.S. Navy Submarine Force Museum. *Submarine*. New York: DK Publishing, 2003.

Marine Life Books

- Andreae, Giles. *Commotion in the Ocean.* Illustrated by David Wojtowycz. Wilton, CT: Tiger Tales, 2002. A collection of silly verses about various creatures that live in the ocean.

- Roberts, Bethany. *Follow Me!* Illustrated by Diane Greenseid. New York: Clarion Books, 1998. A mother octopus leads her little ones past all sorts of sea creatures as they make their way through the underwater world.

Marine Life Books for Children to Browse

- Galloway, Ruth. *Fidgety Fish.* Wilton, CT: Tiger Tales, 2001. Sent out for a swim in the deep sea, Tiddler, a young fish who just can't keep still, sees many interesting creatures and one very dark cave.

- Rose, Deborah Lee. *Into the A, B, Sea: An Ocean Alphabet.* Illustrations by Steve Jenkins. New York: Scholastic Press, 2000.

- Ross, Kathy. *Crafts for Kids Who Are Wild about Oceans.* Illustrated by Sharon Lane Holm. Brookfield, CT: Millbrook Press, 1998. For program follow up; provides instructions for using common household materials to make fish, sea urchins, a sea turtle, and other ocean creatures for toys, decoration, or science projects.

Music

- "Malibu Surf" and ocean sounds, from *Hush little Baby: Soothing Sounds for Sleep.* Pacific Palisades, CA: Kids Music Factory, 2003.

- "Octopus's Garden" and "Yellow Submarine," from *All You Need Is Love: [Beatles Songs for Kids].* Redway, CA: Music for Little People, 1999.

Space Needs

- Approximately 2 square feet of space for each child, carpeted or hard floor

Materials and Equipment

- CD and cassette player

- Drum and drumsticks or empty oatmeal container and two chopsticks taped together

- Metal percussion instrument (triangle or metal chimes that you can strike) or metal can and table utensil

- Basket or bag

- Slips of folded paper with the names on them of the marine animals from the book *Commotion in the Ocean.* Make a double set; they will work in partners.

- Two sets of pictures of the animals from the same book with poem

- Poster paper with the word "commotion" on it

Before You Begin

- Gather all materials.

- Review and practice the program.

Program

Introduction

> Our program today is called "Ocean's Alive." Today we are going to board a yellow submarine, which will take us deep under the ocean. We will see all kinds of plants and animals that live in the sea.

Story and Movement Time

Part 1: What Is a Submarine? (10 Minutes)

Leader: *Does anyone know what a submarine is?* [Encourage answers. Have children browse books on submarines. Read and show pictures from *Rub-a-Dub Sub*.]

Part 2: Marching to the Submarine (5 Minutes)

Ask children to form a double line on one side of the room. They will be marching around all four sides of the room.

Leader: *Let's all march to the yellow submarine for our voyage under the sea. Say "Let's all march to the yellow submarine," as you march.*

Movement: Strike the drum on the first of every four counts, counting to three before you strike the drum again. Repeat as the children march around all four sides of the room. Have them clap on the first count, as you hit the drum. This is a four-count march rhythm with the emphasis on the first count.

Part 3: Shimmy Down (5 Minutes)

Leader: *Stop! Freeze! We've arrived; let's open the hatch and shimmy down to the inside of the submarine. Say "Shimmy down" several times as you enter the submarine.*

Movement: Quickly strike three counts on the metal percussion instrument, one strike for each beat; repeat six times. Have them say "shim-my-down" for each three counts. Pinch your nostrils and shimmy down, bending your knees. Repeat the shimmy down six times.

Play the "Yellow Submarine" song.

Have children do dance improvisation to the song, including the shimmy down movement.

Part 4: Marine Animals Deep Under the Sea (25 Minutes)

Have children browse marine animal books. Show the poster board with the word "commotion" on it. A *commotion* is a condition of turbulent motion, a disturbance or disruption. Pronounce it with the children and read the definition.

Read and show pictures from *Commotion in the Ocean*. Have the children choose a slip of paper from the basket with the name of an animal from the book. Give them the picture and poem of their animals. They are not expected to be able to read the poem; they can take it home and practice the activity with their families later. Have them work with a partner, the other person who chooses that animal. Have them practice the basic animal movements based on their shapes as they observe them in the pictures from the book. After the program they may wish to practice reading the poem with you. The movement they've done will reinforce their understanding of the text.

Form a circle of children, pretending to be looking out a porthole (toward the center of the circle) and seeing the animals in the poems. One pair of children at a time dances at the center of the circle to one of the poems, as you read the rhymes aloud to accompany the children's movement; the others copy their dance or just watch.

Read *Follow Me!* Have the children move spontaneously as you read. The story is written in a simple rhyme format.

Play "Octopus's Garden." The children may do their free-form movement.

Part 5: Surfacing and Debarking (10 Minutes)

Leader: *We are slowly rising up to the surface of the sea*

Movement: Have everyone line up, holding onto their neighbor's shoulder, and rise up slowly onto the balls of their feet.

Leader: *Rising higher and higher*

Movement: Stay up there and rise even higher, right out of your body.

Leader: *We've returned to the surface of the sea; let's shimmy up, instead of down, can you do that? Where would you start?*

Movement: Everyone's knees should be deeply bent and they should shimmy up to standing flat on their feet.

Leader: *Let's open the hatch and step out onto the dock, where we started; we are back home.*

Movement: This can be improvised.

Program 5: Arroyo Loco—A Crazy StoryTrip to the Mexican Desert

Summary

Traveling by dirt bikes to the desert in Mexico, the children visit Señor Coyote, who is running and hiding from the dogs. The children re-create the story, running across the desert and leaping over the arroyo, and do a circle dance, with Coyote in the center *cueva* and the dogs pawing and whining from the outside. They explore desert animals and plants and improvise movements to poems under the burning sun; it's hot, *mucho caliente!* This program takes about one and a half hours, including the show-and-tell introduction.

Program Preparation

Books

- Bash, Barbara. *Desert Giant: The World of the Saguaro Cactus.* San Francisco: Sierra Club Books; Boston: Little, Brown, 1989. Documents the life cycle and ecosystem of the giant saguaro cactus and the desert animals it helps to support.

- "Coyote and the Dogs." In Pat Nelson. *Magic Minutes*: *Quick Read-Alouds for Every Day.* Illustrated by Kath B. Gordon. Englewood, CO: Libraries Unlimited, 1993; or "Coyote and the Dogs." In Dan Storm. *Picture Tales from Mexico.* Illustrations by Mark Storm. New York: Frederick A. Stokes, 1941.

- Greenberg, David T. *Snakes!* Illustrated by Lynn Munsinger. New York: Little, Brown, 2004. A rhyming snake story

- Taylor Barbara, and Mark O'Shea. *Reptiles: A World Guide to Snakes, Lizards, Turtles, Tortoises, Crocodiles and Alligators.* London: Lorenz, 2004.

Other Desert Books

- Johnston, Tony. *Desert Song.* Illustrations by Ed Young. San Francisco: Sierra Club Books for Children, 2000. As the heat of the desert day fades into night, various nocturnal animals, including bats, coyotes, and snakes, venture out to find food.

- Levinson, Nancy Smiler. *Death Valley: A Day in the Desert.* Illustrated by Diane Dawson Hearn. New York: Holiday House, 2001.

- Pallotta, Jerry. *The Desert Alphabet.* Illustrated by Mark Astrella. Watertown, MA: Charlesbridge, 1994.

- Steiner, Barbara. *Desert Trip.* Illustrations by Ronald Himler. San Francisco: Sierra Club Books for Children, 1996. Relates the experiences of a young girl and her mother as they backpack in the desert, where the child learns about the plants, animals, birds, and rock formations.

Music

- Bo Diddley. "Road Runner," from *Bo Diddley.* Universal City, CA: MCA Records, 2000; or

- Sugar Beats. "Road Runner," from *Car Tunes.* New York: Sugar Beats Entertainment, 2000; or

- The Who. "Road Runner," from *Who's Next?* Universal City, CA: MCA Records, 1995.

Space Needs

- Carpeted or smooth open movement space, at least 20 feet by 20 feet, for 20 children

Materials and Equipment

- CD and cassette player

- Computer and computer projector for pictures (optional)

- Pictures of a desert, an arroyo in the desert, a road runner, a dirt bike, a desert coyote, a rattlesnake, a saguaro cactus, and a lizard. Web sites for pictures are listed at the end of this chapter.

- Empty plastic eggshells and unshelled brown rice, one shell for each child and one tablespoon of rice for each shell

- "Arroyo Loco Vocabulary List" (at end of chapter)

Before You Begin

- Gather all equipment and materials.

- Decide on the method for showing the pictures. (Pictures can be projected from computer or shown from books or downloaded from Web pages.) Gather the equipment, pictures, or books that you need.

- Review and practice the program.

- Change the names of the coyote's paws, ears, eyes, and tail to Spanish words from the vocabulary list.

Program

Introduction

> [Review the vocabulary list. This is a show-and-tell activity. Show the pictures and teach the children the meanings and pronunciations of the Spanish words.] *Our "Dance-About" program today is called "Arroyo Loco—A Crazy Trip to the Mexican Desert." We are going to the desert to visit a coyote, some dogs, a rattlesnake, a saguaro cactus, and a lizard. And now we must be on our way!*

Story and Movement Time

Part 1: Dirt Biking to the Desert (10 Minutes)

Leader: *We are going to travel to the desert on dirt bikes! Before I turn on the music, let's practice riding our dirt bikes.* [They should start moving forward at Step 4; make sure everyone is moving from one side of the moving space to the other.]

1. Leader: *Revving up the dirt bike engine*

Movement: Grasp the handles of an imaginary bike, then squeeze and partially release your hands several times, leaning forward from the hips at a 45 degree angle.

2. Leader: *The bike rumbles.*

Movement: Vibrate your body, with elbows extended and arms quickly fluttering while grasping the "handles."

3. Leader: *Release the break.*

Movement: Flip your right foot back, bending your right knee.

4. Leader: *Step on it.*

Movement: Squeeze the "handles" and run.

5. Leader: *Over a small rock, do a small wheelie*

Movement: Lean back slightly and raise your arms, squeezing your hands, and lean forward.

6. Leader: *Going through the arroyo*

Movement: Lean forward with our head in line with your body.

7. Leader: *Going straight*

Movement: Run forward.

8. Leader: *Going around a bend to the right*

Movement: Shift your weight to the right.

9. Leader: *Going around a bend to the left*

Movement: Shift your weight to the left.

Repeat steps 8 and 9 a few times.

10. Leader: *Going over medium rock, do a large wheelie*

Movement: Lean way back and raise your arms, squeeze your hands, and lunge forward.

11. Leader: *Flying over the arroyo*

Movement: Bend your knees and leap from one foot to the next. Land on a bent knee.

Play the "Road Runner" song.

Repeat the movements; model them without verbal directions.

Part 2: Coyote and the Dogs (5 Minutes)

Read or tell "Coyote and the Dogs" with the substituted Spanish names for the parts of the coyote's body.

Part 3: The Chase (15 Minutes)

Divide the children into two groups, with each group having coyotes and dogs. Put each group in half of the movement space. Remind them that they shouldn't push, shove, or pull each other. Ask children to make up movements to the following images:

Leader:

1. Coyotes walk, care free, in the desert.

2. Half of the dogs spring out from behind some bushes.

3. The dogs chase the coyotes around the bushes and over rocks, leaping over arroyos.

4. The coyotes run away and can hear the dogs yelping from a distance.

5. The coyotes can't decide where to hide.

6. The other half of the dogs spring out of the rocks in front of them.

7. The coyotes run back and forth between the two sets of dogs chasing them.

8. The coyotes turn and run until they find a cueva, *a cave; they jump into the* cueva.

9. The dogs yelp and snap at the coyotes' colas *(tails).*

Part 4: Gone to the Dogs (10 Minutes)

Have coyotes in the *cueva* in the center of the circle. The dogs form the circle around the coyotes, periodically whining softly and pawing the ground. All are seated on the floor as Señor Coyote talks to the parts of their bodies. Ask the coyotes to answer the questions and create a little dance at the same time that they answer.

1. Leader: *What does Señor Coyote say to his* patas, *his feet?*

Movement: Have the coyotes do a dance showing off their feet and say what he said to his feet as they dance.

2. Leader: *What does Señor Coyote say to his* orejas, *his ears?*

Movement: Have the coyotes do a dance showing off their ears and say what he said to his ears as they dance.

3. Leader: *What does Señor Coyote say to his* ojos, *his eyes?*

Movement: Have the coyotes do a dance showing off their eyes and say what he said to his eyes as they dance.

4. Leader: *What does Señor Coyote say to his* cola, *his tail?*

Movement: Have the coyotes push their tails out of the cave as they scold their tails. All the dogs yelp and snap (there should be no actual touching).

Part 5: Snakes (20 Minutes)

Read *Snakes!*

Read a few pages from *Desert Giant: The World of the Saguaro Cactus*, about birds living inside them.

Read a few pages on lizards from *Reptiles: A World Guide to Snakes, Lizards, Turtles, Tortoises, Crocodiles and Alligators.*

Leader: *Here come the Rattlesnakes; let's do the Rattlesnake Rock.* [Have children fill the empty eggs with the rice to use as rattlers. Have them improvise movement and shake the rattles as you recite the poem below. They can be standing and change levels; it is best not to be on the floor the whole time, as it limits the potential for movement.]

The Rattlesnake Rock (original poem)

> **Leader:** *I slither to the right.*
>
> *I slither to the left.*
>
> *I rattle all around.*
>
> *And I make a hissing sound: Hisssssss!*
>
> Repeat several times.

Part 6: Cacti (5 minutes)

Leader: *Look out, don't run into **that** tree; it's a cactus! It's sharp!* [Recite the following and let the children make up movements to the images.]

I Am a Cactus (original poem)

> **Leader:** *I am a Cactus,*
>
> *straight and tall*
>
> *In the desert,*
>
> *nobody bothers me at all.*
>
> *I have prickly spines,*
>
> *that make you go ouch!*
>
> *I am a cactus,*
>
> *I'm no slouch.*
>
> *A bird moved inside me,*
>
> *I don't know when.*
>
> *She only says,*
>
> *"I'm a wren."*

Part 7: Lizards (5 Minutes)

Leader: *It's hot out here in the desert sun; it must be 120 degrees, but Hank the lizard doesn't mind.* [Recite the following and let the children make up movements to the images.]

Hank, the Lizard (original poem)

> **Leader:** *May I introduce you to a lizard named Hank,*
>
> *Not Bill, Jerry, or Frank*
>
> *His name is Hank.*
>
> *All day, he lies in the sun*
>
> *For him, that is a lot of fun!*

Part 8: Ride Dirt Bikes Home (5 Minutes)

Leader: *Whew! It's hot,* mucho caliente*! Let's hop on our dirt bikes and buzz on home!* [Play the "Road Runner" song and let children improvise movements.]

Teaching Resource

Arroyo Loco Vocabulary List

Arroyo = A dry desert gully, usually a small, narrow canyon with steep walls and a flat, gravel strewn floor. Picture available at http://www2.mcdaniel.edu/Biology/wildamerica/desert/desertgeolgy.html.

Cola = tail

Cueva = cave

Loco = slang for insane or crazy

Ojos = eyes (j is pronounced like an h)

Orejas = ears (j is pronounced like an h)

Patas = paws

Web Sites for Pictures

Cactus wren. A bird that makes its home in cacti. Picture available at http://www.terragalleria.com/pictures-subjects/outside/picture.outside.usaz33522.html.

Coyote. A wild canine related to the wolf.

Picture available at http://www.desertusa.com/june96/du_cycot.html.

Desert. A geographical area receiving less than 10 inches of precipitation (rain) annually. Picture available at http://www.odysseyphoto.com/portfolio/Mexico/Mexico-Baja.html.

Dirt bikes. Hardy off-road bikes used in the desert and other difficult terrain. Picture available at http://www.midgetmotorsports.com.

Lizard. A relatively long-bodied reptile with usually two pairs of legs and a tapering tail. Picture available at http://www.southalley.com/lizard_oax.html.

Rattlesnake. A venomous snake. Picture available at http://www.desertusa.com/may96/du_rattle.html.

Road runner. A bird that runs very quickly across the desert. Picture available at http://www.scsc.k12.ar.us/2000TexNatHist/TexasNatHist/Members/LachowskyR/runners.jpg.

Saguaro cactus. A treelike cactus that provides homes for desert birds, such as the cactus wren. Picture available at http://helios.bto.ed.ac.uk/bto/desbiome/saguaro.htm#top http://www.desertusa.com/mag03/nov/desertfea.html.

Chapter 4

StoryTrip Programs: Ages Six to Eight

Introduction

StoryTrip™ programs encourage problem solving through role-playing real-life situations that come up in stories. In re-creating the story, children have the opportunity to experience alternative solutions and consequential thinking. With their ability to follow directions, they are guided through the story sequence as they learn character dialogue and movement. By interacting as characters, they develop intellectually and socially and understand the feelings of others. They develop literacy skills by expanding their vocabulary and grammatical abilities. They are able to translate feelings into movement, increasing their movement (nonverbal) vocabulary. Using their imagination in response to suggested imagery, they improvise dialogue and movement.

If the leader of the program does not have a background in storytelling and wishes to perform the literature, see the handout "Trigger Method of Learning a Story (Group Leader)," at the end of chapter 6.

Children participate in choreographed cultural dances as they mirror movements created by the leader. They develop cultural literacy about another country by learning a few words in the language of that country, some of its history and customs, and a cultural dance. Details about six-to-eight-year-olds' cognitive and physical skills are outlined in Table 4.1.

Table 4.1. Readiness to Learn (6- to 8-Year-Olds)

COGNITIVE	PHYSICAL
➢ Beginnings of logical thought ➢ Beginnings of concrete problem solving ➢ Beginnings of social speech ➢ Understanding of story structure and elements ➢ Awareness of other countries (cultural literacy) ➢ Awareness of past and future ➢ Ability to follow directions ➢ Alternative solutions and consequences ➢ Understanding of feelings of others ➢ Ability to retell plots and practice dialogue ➢ Expanded knowledge of word meanings and relations, refining of grammar	➢ Some improvisational movement of characters, settings, and events ➢ Simple choreographed folk dances ➢ Ability to do imitative movement, mirroring what leader is doing

Program 1: StoryTrip to Mexico

Summary

After hearing the story *Borreguita and the Coyote,* children hop on and become the "Train of Imagination" on a journey to Mexico. Train stops include the VocHotel, where they learn character voices and improvise dialogue, and the MoveInn, where they learn character movement. When they reach their destination, the Farm at the Foot of the Mountain, they reenact the story with improvised twists. They celebrate by dancing The Mexican Hat Dance at a fiesta before they take the train home. The program takes about 60 to 80 minutes, depending on how much they change the story and improvise. Ten minutes is included for the introduction.

Program Preparation

Books

Story Selection

- Aardema, Verna. *Borreguita and the Coyote: A Tale from Ayutla, Mexico.* Illustrated by Petra Mathers. New York: Knopf, distributed by Random House, 1991. A little lamb uses her clever wiles to keep a coyote from eating her up.

Books for Children to Browse

Mexico

- Berendes, Mary. *Mexico.* [Plymouth, MN]: Child's World, 1998.

- Krebs, Laurie. *Off We Go to Mexico: An Adventure in the Sun.* Illustrated by Christopher Corr. Cambridge, MA: Barefoot Books, 2006.

- Tabor, Nancy Maria Grande. *Celebrations: Holidays of the United States of America and Mexico = Celebraciones: dias feriados de los Estados Unidos y Mixico.* Watertown, MA: Charlesbridge, 2003.

Coyotes

- Hodge, Deborah. *Wild Dogs: Wolves, Coyotes and Foxes.* Illustrated by Pat Stephens. Toronto: Kids Can Press, 1997.

- Lepthien, Emilie U. *Coyotes.* Chicago: Children's Press, 1993.

- Swanson, Diane. *Welcome to the World of Coyotes.* Vancouver: Whitecap Books, 2001.

Music

Train Music

- "A Train Ride," from *Hush Little Baby: Soothing Sounds for Sleep.* Pacific Palisades, CA: Kids Music Factory, 2003.

- William Eaton Ensemble. "Midsummer Night's Fever," from *Where Rivers Meet.* Phoenix: Wisdom Tree Music, distributed by Canyon Records, 1994.

Mexican Hat Dance

- *Bailes favoritos: de todos los tiempos = All-time Favorite Dances.* Long Branch, NJ: Kimbo Educational, [2003?].

- Stewart, Georgiana Liccione. *Folk Dance Fun: Simpler Folk Songs & Dances.* Long Branch, NJ: Kimbo Educational, 1984.

Space Needs

- Open movement space of about 2 to 3 square feet per child, uncarpeted

Materials and Equipment

- CD and cassette player

- Percussion instrument (e.g., a flat hand drum and drum stick or sealed oatmeal box and large wooden spoon)

- Sombrero or other wide-brimmed hat

- Ten to twenty feet of brightly colored 1-inch masking tape to tape to the floor in the Farm at the Foot of the Mountain section of the program
- Globe or world map

Before You Begin

- Make a copy of the "StoryTrip to Mexico Vocabulary List" handout (at end of this section) for each child.
- Gather materials and equipment.
- Read or browse the books and practice the program.

Program

Introduction

> Welcome, children to the "PresentStation." After we hear a story today, we will board and *become* the train for a StoryTrip to Mexico. We will visit the VocHotel, the MoveInn, and the Farm at the Foot of the Mountain. All of you get to be storytellers today. First we're going to learn a bit about the country of Mexico.

Browse books on Mexico with the children and show the location of Mexico on the globe or world map. Give them the "StoryTrip to Mexico Vocabulary List" handout. Go over the words and their pronunciation. Have children repeat the words. Browse the nonfiction books on coyotes so that they can distinguish a coyote from a dog or wolf.

Story Presentation (10 Minutes)

Play just the first couple of notes of trainlike sounds in the piece "Midsummer Night's Fever." Rewind and replay it upon boarding the train of imagination, after the story.

Read or tell *Borreguita and the Coyote: A Tale from Ayutla, Mexico.*

Story Vocal and Movement Exercises (60 Minutes)

Part 1: The Train Trip (10 Minutes)

Play "Midsummer Night's Fever." Stop the tape at the point the children put on their brakes (see below). Rewind for the return train trip at the end of the program.

Leader: *Here comes the train.* [Have the children form a circle and turn to the right and walk behind each other clockwise one round for each instruction, except when they go "around the bends." Take your place behind a child in the circle. Call out the images and demonstrate the movements. The images to be called out are as follows:]

1. Leader: *Stepping high onto the train.*

Movement: Step high in place.

2. Leader: *Now you are the train.*

3. Leader: *The train is getting ready to take off; it is vibrating.*

Movement: Vibrate or shake your whole body.

4. Leader: *Here we go! The train is moving forward.*

Movement: Move forward.

5. Leader: *The wheels are churning round and round. Chug, Chug.*

Movement: Walk in the circle with your arms bent at the elbows, circling your shoulders and saying chug, chug.

5. Leader: *The train is going up a mountain. Reach up high, stretch.*

Movement: Walk, looking up and stretching your arms over your head.

6. Leader: *The train is going down into a valley. A deep valley.*

Movement: Place your arms on the shoulders of the person in front of you and walk with bent knees.

7. Leader: *The train is going around a bend to the right.*

Movement: Stand in place and turn around several times to the right.

8. Leader: *Around a bend to the left.*

Movement: Stand in place and turn around several times to the left.

9. Leader: *The train is going back up a mountain.*

Movement: Walk and reach up high.

10. Leader: *Passing through a narrow tunnel.*

Movement: Hold your arms straight down tightly at your sides.

11. Leader: *We've arrived at the VocHotel. The train is coming to a halt, everyone, put on your brakes.*

Movement: Make a braking sound and halting movement.

Part 2: VocHotel (10 Minutes)

Leader: *We have arrived in Mexico: First we will visit The VocHotel. The voices of Borreguita and Coyote are waiting inside for us.*

Divide the class in half. One half will be Borreguitas and the other half will be Señor Coyotes. Seat the Borreguitas in a row facing the Coyotes, about 4 feet apart. Take your place at the head of the rows, midway between them. Encourage children to use the correct pronunciation and character voices. It is best if they raise their hands, so that one person at a time is speaking and more than one person can be called on to fill in the blanks.

Leader: *Please raise your hand to fill in the blanks: On a farm in Ayutla, Mexico, lived a little ewe lamb. Her name was* _____. *As she was eating clover, along came* _____. *And Señor Coyote said, "Grrr! Borreguita you look delicious and I am* _____! *And Borreguita answered Baa-a-a, Baa-a-a! Oh, Señor Coyote, I am* _____. *After I eat some more, I will be* _____. *Come back* _____. *And what did the coyote say? A couple of days later, Señor Coyote returned. What did he say then? And what did Borreguita tell him? Did Coyote want to eat some cheese? Where did Borreguita tell him to meet her to get a cheese?*

Part 3: Changing the Story (10 Minutes)

Have the children take turns or raise their hands to answer some questions.

Leader: *When you give your answer, I want you to stand up and project your voice across the room, so everyone can hear you.* [Ask the following plot questions:]

    1. Leader: *What else could Borreguita have said or done to keep Coyote from eating her?*

    2. Leader: *What would coyote have said or done then?*

    3. Leader: *What would happen next?* [Repeat this question as long as there are answers coming from the children or until you feel it's time to move on to the ending.]

    4. Leader: *How does your story end?*

    5. Leader: *Does anyone else have another ending?* [Repeat this question as long as there are answers coming from the children or until you feel it's time to finish.]

Part 4: MoveInn (10 Minutes)

Leader: *Next we are going to visit the MoveInn. Borreguita and Señor Coyote are waiting inside to show us how they move.*

Have the children line up in rows of three or four, side-by-side, arm's length apart, to move across the floor, Borreguitas go first, followed by Coyotes, to the following beats and images:

Señor Coyote and Borreguita Line Up.

Leader: *Borreguitas: Walk very quickly and take small and light steps.* [Play this rhythm on your drum: 1-and-2 and repeat, striking on the number and say "and" to yourself between beats.]

You are very clever and tricked that coyote again. Leap and hop lightly and smile and laugh across the floor. [The Borreguitas go first across the floor. They are at the other end when the Coyotes start.]

Coyotes: You are prowling; walk very slowly and take very big and heavy steps. Bend your knees deeply when you walk, like you are prowling. [Play this rhythm on your drum: 1-e-and-a, 2-e-and-a, and repeat, only striking the instrument on the numbers; say "e-and-a" to yourself between beats.] *You are very hungry; think of your favorite food or a delicious lamb. Lick your chops. Remember to bend your knees as you walk.*

Part 5: The Farm at the Foot of the Mountain (10–15 Minutes)

Create a center line on the floor with the brightly colored tape. Have the coyotes on one side of the line and the Borreguitas on the other. Tell the children the rules for the improvisation.

Leader: *Now we are at the Farm at the Foot of the Mountain, where we will use our character voices and movements to re-create the story.* [For the following, you can either use the sequence of events of the story that you read or told, use the ones that the children made up in Part 3—or make up new incidents on the spot.]
These are the rules:

- *Coyotes and Borreguitas are to stay on their own side of the line; please, no reaching over the line.*

- *Move in an upright position: do not go down to the floor; do not go down on all fours. You are storytellers acting as animals; you are not the animals.*

We are at the Farm at the foot of the mountain in Ayutla, Mexico. Borreguita is eating clover in the meadow. Borreguitas, make up some light steps, as you eat clover in the meadow, on your side of the line. [Play the Borreguita rhythm for a few minutes, as the Borreguitas dance.]

Here comes Señor Coyote. Coyotes, make up some prowling steps as you approach Borreguita, but stay on your side of the line. [Play the Coyote rhythm for a few minutes as the Coyotes prowl.]

Choose one child at a time to lead in playing follow-the-leader. Whatever that child says and however that child moves must be copied by the other Coyotes or Borreguitas. Remind them to stay on their own side of the line. Play the Coyote rhythms when they are speaking and moving and the Borreguita rhythms when they are speaking and moving.

Leader: *What does Coyote say to Borreguita? What does Borreguita reply? What happens when Coyote returns? Show him prowling back. What does Borreguita offer him instead of lamb? What happens after that? You can use the changes in the story that you made at the VocHotel if you wish.*
And how does it end?

Part 6: Fiesta (5–10 Minutes)

Leader: *Let's go to a fiesta and celebrate Borreguita's freedom.* [Before putting on the music, teach them the following Mexican Hat Dance:]

1. Form a circle, holding hands. [Place the sombrero in the middle of the circle.]

2. Put your hands on your hips.

3. Extend your right heel (a slight jump) in front of you, then return your right foot.

Mexican Hat Dance.

4. Extend your left heel in front of you (a slight jump), then return your left foot

5. Extend your right heel in front of you (a slight jump), clap your hands, return your right foot

6. Repeat steps 3 through 5, eight more times to the music

7. Hold hands and circle round [music changes].

8. Repeat steps 2 through 7 and circle in the other direction.

[Play the "Mexican Hat Dance" song and have the children do the above dance to the music, one or more times. It is a fun dance that most children enjoy doing.]

Part 7: The Train Ride Home (5 Minutes)

Repeat the train ride movement at the beginning of the program, using the same music.

StoryTrip to Mexico Vocabulary List (Transliterated)

Ayutla (ah yoot la). Ayutla de los Libres (Ayutla of the Free). The commercial center for an agricultural, cattle-raising, and lumbering area. The Plan of Ayutla, drawn up in 1854, was a reform program intended to remove the dictator Santa Anna and convening a constituent assembly to frame a federal constitution. It is located on the western coast of Mexico.

Borreguita (boh-rray-GEE-tah). Little lamb.

Coyote. A small wolflike carnivore, native to western North America and found in many other regions of the continent. Also called prairie wolf.

Está bien (es tah b yen). That is good.

Fiesta (fee es ta). A festival or religious holiday, especially a saint's day, celebrated in Spanish-speaking countries.

Mexico (meh hee koh). A North American country located south of the United States.

Señor (seh nyor). A Spanish title of respect for a man; equivalent to the English "Mr."

Sombrero (sum brar o). A large straw or felt hat with a broad brim and tall crown, worn especially in Mexico and the American Southwest.

From *Stories on the Move: Integrating Literature and Movement with Children, Infants to Age 14* by Arlene Cohen. Illustrated by Andrea Fitcha McAllister. Westport, CT: Libraries Unlimited. Copyright © 2007.

Program 2: StoryTrip to Africa

Summary

After hearing the story "Anansi the Spider's Hat Shaking Dance," the children paddle canoes up the Volta River and become the Vessels to the grasslands of Ghana. On the river, they encounter hippopotami and mosquitoes. In Ghana, at the VocHut, they learn the character voices and improvise a Hat Shaking Dance at the CopaSavannah Night Club. The children learn a lively funeral dance from Ghana along with story-related vocabulary. They make traditional African hats before they paddle to Ghana. This program lasts about 80 minutes, depending on the improvisational variations and including 10 minutes for the introduction.

Program Preparation

Books

Hat Shaking Dance Stories

- Cole, Joanna, selector. "The Hat-Shaking Dance." In *Best-Loved Folktales of the World*. Illustrated by Jill Karla Schwarz. Garden City, NY: Doubleday, 1982.

- Courlander, Harold, with Albert Kofi Prempeh. *The Hat-Shaking Dance, and Other Ashanti Tales from Ghana*. Illustrated by Enrico Arno. New York: Harcourt, Brace & World, 1957. Anansi the Spider, an African trickster, tries to impress his friends by appearing too sad to eat at his mother-in-law's funeral. When he gets very hungry, he spills the beans.

- Eagle Horse, Chris, reteller. *Anansi's Hat-Shaking Dance—An Ashanti Folk Tale from Africa*. Jeffco Multicultural Lesson Plans. Golden, CO: Jeffco Public Schools, n.d. Available at http://jeffcoweb.jeffco.k12.co.us/passport/lessonplan/lessons/trickster.html.

- Powell, Megan. "How Anansi Lost His Hair." In *Fables: The Home of Folktales and Speculative Fiction on the Internet*. 1998. Available at http://www.fables.org/crown_thistle/hair.html.

Books on Ghana

- La Pierre, Yvette. *Ghana in Pictures*. Minneapolis, MN: Lerner Publications, 2004. Through text and photographs introduces the land, history, government, people, and economy of Ghana. Shows maps with Volta River.

- Levy, Patricia. *Ghana*. New York: Marshall Cavendish, 1999. Describes the geography, history, government, economy, people, lifestyle, religion, language, arts, leisure, festivals, and food of Ghana. Shows map with Volta River.

Music

- Recordings of jungle sounds, such as those found on:

  - *Animals and Birds* [Cuts 43-46]. Princeton, NJ: Films for the Humanities & Sciences, [1991], 1986.

  - *Jungle Talk: The Natural Sounds of the Wilderness* [Side A]. Santa Monica, CA: LaserLight, 1993.

- Robert Duskis, comp. "Sidudla" by Mabi Thobejane and "Can Gna" by Les Go, from *African Travels*. San Francisco: Six Degrees Records, 2001.

Space Needs

- Open uncarpeted space with approximately 2 to 3 square feet for each child.

- Tables and chairs that can be easily moved to the side for the craft project.

Materials and Equipment

- CD and cassette player

- Handout: "StoryTrip to Africa Vocabulary List" (at end of section)

- Crayons and 20 lb., 8½-by-11-inch, brightly colored paper and 1-inch wide tape for each child to make paper hats

- Preschool style scissors, one for every two children to share or one for each child

- Globe or world map

- Map of Ghana, showing Volta River (see Web site below)

Before You Begin

- Make copies of the handouts for each child: "StoryTrip to Africa Vocabulary List" (the list appears twice on the handout so you can cut the copy in half and provide for two children from each copy) and "Anansi the Spider's Hat Pattern Instructions" (at end of this section; the instructions appear twice on the handout so you can cut the copy in half and provide for two children from each copy).

- Print out a map of Ghana from http://www.cia.gov/cia/publications/factbook/index. html.

- Reproduce the paper hat patterns (Figures 4.1 and 4.2). (Sample African hats can be viewed at http://www.rebirth.co.za/african_hats.htm) or in the books on Ghana.

- Review and practice the program.

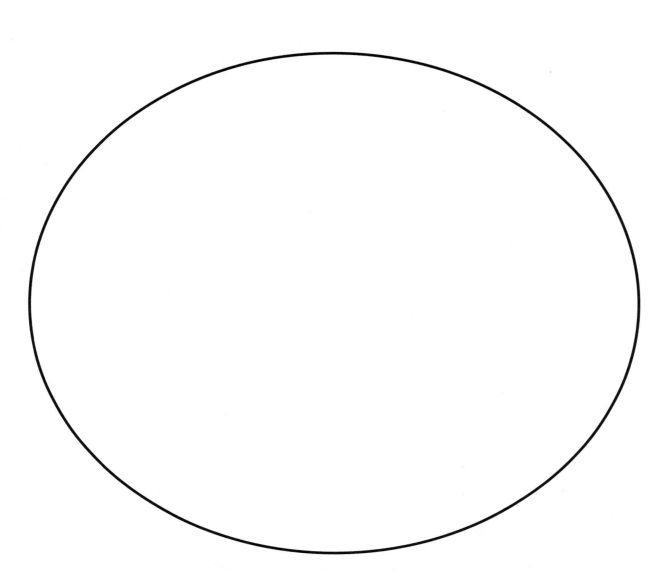

Figure 4.1. Anansi the Spider's Hat Pattern—Top.

Figure 4.2. Anansi the Spider's Hat Pattern—Side Strip.

Program

Introduction

> Welcome to the boat dock. After we hear a story today, we will paddle canoes up the Volta River and *become* the canoes for a "StoryTrip to Africa." But first let's learn a bit about Ghana, a country on the continent of Africa. [Distribute the vocabulary list handout and explain that Ghana is a country in Western Africa. Show the location of Africa on the globe or world map. Point to the Volta River on the map of Ghana that you have printed out. Review the words on the vocabulary page, having children repeat the words after you.] *Now, to get ready, we are going to make some traditional African hats.*

Paper Hat Project (10 Minutes)

Give children the "Anansi the Spider's Hat Pattern Instructions" handout from the end of this program.

Story Presentation (10 Minutes)

Play just the first couple of notes of animal sounds, cuts 43–46 from *Animals and Birds.*

Leader: *It is common for close relatives of the deceased in the Ashanti Tribe to vent their grief through wailing and tears. Anansi the Spider was far from being an exception to that custom.*

Read or tell one of the versions of the "The Hat-Shaking Dance" story.

Story Vocal and Movement Exercises (60–75 Minutes)

Part 1: The Canoe Trip (10 Minutes)

To set the mood, play background jungle sounds. Assemble the children on one of the long sides of the movement space, facing the center of the space. Then point to the center of the space.

Leader:

- *There are the canoes; there are four of them over there on the shore. Let's divide into groups of four.* [Adjust the numbers so you have approximately four groups.]
- *Pick up your paddles and place them in the canoe.*
- *There is the Volta River, which is about 15 feet beyond the boats; can you see it?*
- *With your group, drag a canoe into the river.*
- *Now you are going to board and* ***become*** *vessels of imagination for our trip to Ghana, Africa. Step into the canoe; be careful not to tip it, and keep your balance.*

- *Now you **are** the vessels of imagination. Arrange your paddles. Squat or bend forward slightly, but don't sit down, because it will be easier to move.*

- *Now we're going to paddle through the river. Remember to stay with the rest of group that you are in, in your position within the boat. Let's go. Paddle up the river.*

- *Uh, oh, we went the wrong way! Turn the boat around by paddling and go the other way.*

- *Uh-oh, there is a large family of hippopotami in the middle of the river! We'd better go around them. They are all over the place.*

- *Oh no! Now there's a swarm of mosquitoes—they're everywhere! Swat them with your paddles!*

- *We'd better paddle out of this, as quickly as possible.*

- *Here we are—we've finally arrived at Anansi's village in Ghana, in the grasslands of Africa. Let's pull our boats onto shore.*

Part 2: The VocHut (10–15 Minutes)

Leader: *We have arrived in Ghana. First we will visit the VocHut. Listen—Anansi the Spider and his friends are waiting inside for us.*

Divide the class in half. One half will play the part of Anansi, and the other half will play Anansi's friends. Seat the Anansi players in a row, either on the floor or on chairs, facing the friends, about 4 feet apart. Take your place at the head of the rows, midway between the rows.

Leader: *Please take turns in answering the following questions. I will call on you, one by one. When I call on you, please stand up, project your voice across the room, and pretend that you are the character.*

- *Anansi, what did you eat before you left for the funeral?* [Ask this question of each child that is playing the part of Anansi.]

- *After the funeral, there was a big feast. Anansi's friends thought he would eat like everyone else, but Anansi refused to eat. They tried to encourage him to eat. What did they say to him?* [Ask this question of each child that is playing the part of a friend.]

- *What did Anansi do and say to show that he was just too, too, sad to eat?* [Ask this question of each child that is playing the part of Anansi.]

- *What happened when he got very, very hungry?* [Anyone may answer.]

- *How might you change this story so that it ends differently?* [Anyone may answer. You may prompt them, if they don't answer with:] *What if he hadn't stuffed himself before he left home? What if he had eaten like everyone else? What if he hadn't hid the beans in his hat?*

- *Have you ever played a trick on your friends? What trick did you play?* [Anyone may answer.] *Did you get away with it?*

Part 3: The CopaSavannah Night Club (10 Minutes)

Leader: *Next we are going to visit the famous night club, the CopaSavannah. I've heard that it is* **the** **place** *to do the hat-shaking dance.*

Play "Can Gna" and let the children improvise a hat-shaking dance.

Part 4: Funeral Dance from Ghana (10 Minutes)

Leader: *In Ghana, funerals last for many days, with lots of dancing. Now we are going to do a funeral dance for Anansi's mother-in-law. All the mourning has already taken place, so this is a joyful dance.* [Demonstrate to the children some of the movements involved in the dance, as you explain:]

Your arms should be bent and away from your sides. Keep them bent and move them in keeping time with the music. This is a bouncy dance consisting of arms, torso, and legs bouncing by hopping, stomping, jumping, and kicking. Your legs go from stomping close to the ground to jumping up in the air. [Now direct the children in the following funeral dance, demonstrating the movements before doing the actual dance. Form two separate circles, side by side: one with girls; one with boys. In both circles, the children face counterclockwise.]

1. Leader: *Girls start first. Boys stay in your own circle; you will start after the girls make one circumference.*

Movement: The girls walk and pulse forward (lightly bouncing on each foot) several times and then turn to the center of the circle and stomp and pulse or shake, repeat facing forward and facing inside three times. Then they repeat the stomp and pulse to the outside of circle, after the forward movement. They should let their bent arms pulse with the rest of their bodies' bouncing to the music.

2. Leader: *Girls, keep moving; do not stop when the boys start.*

3. Leader: *Boys, you're going to run, hop, and jump.*

Movement: Crouching close to the ground, the boys run, then intersperse their strides with three hops and a big jump forward on both feet. This is followed by three jumps up in the air, kicking one leg back with the knee bent.

4. Leader: *Now you girls join in the jumping.*

Movement: The girls also begin jumping forward and up in the air, with both legs kicking backward with bent knees.

Play "Sidudla," by Mabi Thobejane as the children perform the dance they have learned.

Part 5: Paddling Home (5–10 Minutes)

Play background jungle sounds and let the children make up the routine for paddling home.

StoryTrip to Africa Vocabulary List (Transliterated)

Ashanti (ashan te). An African Tribe

Anansi (anan se). A spider who is a trickster in African folktales

Ghana (ga na). A country in West Africa

Volta River (volt a). A river in Ghana.

Trickster. A mischievous or roguish figure in myth or folklore, like the coyote, who typically makes up for physical weakness with cunning and subversive humor. He likes to play tricks.

StoryTrip to Africa Vocabulary List (Transliterated)

Ashanti (ashan te). An African Tribe]

Anansi (anan se). A spider who is a trickster in African folktales

Ghana (ga na). A country in West Africa

Volta River (volt a). A river in Ghana.

Trickster. A mischievous or roguish figure in myth or folklore, like the coyote, who typically makes up for physical weakness with cunning and subversive humor. He likes to play tricks.

Anansi the Spider's Hat Pattern Instructions

1. Cut out round top; make sure it fits the top of your head. Cut some off or make a larger one if it might be too tight or fall off.

2. For strip, fold paper lengthwise in half and cut out. Tape the two strips together on one of the short edges to make one long strip. Cut off or add some if it is too tight or large.

3. Draw and color a pattern on one side of the strip.

4. You can draw some beans on the other side of the strip and on one side of the top, the proposed inside of the top.

5. Wrap the strip around the edge of the top and tape strip to the top.

Anansi the Spider's Hat Pattern Instructions

1. Cut out round top; make sure it fits the top of your head. Cut some off or make a larger one if it might be too tight or fall off.

2. For strip, fold paper lengthwise in half and cut out. Tape the two strips together on one of the short edges to make one long strip. Cut off or add some if it is too tight or large.

3. Draw and color a pattern on one side of the strip.

4. You can draw some beans on the other side of the strip and on one side of the top, the proposed inside of the top.

5. Wrap the strip around the edge of the top and tape strip to the top.

Program 3: StoryTrip to India

Summary

The children take a magic carpet ride to India, via the stars. Before departing, the Genie (the program leader) shows them where India is on the map or globe. Gliding on the magic carpet, they see many things along the way and dance among the stars. They learn about an endangered animal, the Bengal tiger. After hearing *The Tiger Skin Rug* story, the children reenact the story, making up character movement and dialogue. The book, although older, is available from many libraries. The Genie grants them three wishes in the "Make-a-Wish Charade." They do the "Yoga Tiger Pose" on their magic carpet ride home. This program takes about one hour, depending on the improvisations and including the introduction.

Program Preparation

Books

Story Selection

- Rose, Gerald. *The Tiger Skin Rug*. Englewood Cliffs, NJ: Prentice-Hall, 1979. A tiger leaves his home in the jungle and joins a human family, posing as their tiger skin rug.

Alternative Book

- Pitcher, Caroline. *Lord of the Forest*. Illustrated by Jackie Morris. London: Frances Lincoln Children's Books, 2004. After a steadfast search for the lord of the forest, a tiger discovers himself. Takes place in India.

Books for Children to Browse

Tigers

- Kalman, Bobbie. *Endangered Tigers*. New York: Crabtree Publishing, 2004.
- Spilsbury, Richard. *Bengal Tiger: In Danger of Extinction!* Chicago: Heinemann Library, 2004.

India

- Chatterjee, Manini, and Anita Roy. *India*. New York: Dorling Kindersly, 2002.
- Das, Prodeepta. *I Is for India*. London: Frances Lincoln, 1999, 1996.
- Srinivasan, Radhika, and Leslie Jermyn. *India*. New York: Marshall Cavendish, 2002.

Music

- Steppenwolf. "Magic Carpet Ride," from *Steppenwolf.* Universal City, CA: MCA Records, 1999.

Space Needs

- Open movement space of about 2 to 3 square feet per child, smooth floor or carpeted.

Materials and Equipment

- CD and cassette player

- "Magic carpet," 10 by 15 feet; use one of the following: a piece of felt with an oriental pattern and iron-on fringes, a cloth with an oriental pattern with iron-on fringes, a king size bedspread, an area rug, or just imagine a magic carpet on the floor. The size of the "magic carpet" will depend on the number of the children in the program. The children should be an arm's distance from each other, on the carpet. There should be about 3 inches of open space in the area around the magic carpet for movement.

- Handout: "StoryTrip to India Vocabulary List" (at end of this section; the list appears twice on the handout so you can cut the copy in half and provide for two children from each copy).

- Globe or world map

- Genie costume: a towel turban and fancy pin, balloon pants or pajama bottoms gathered with rubber bands near ankles, a paisley print or other colorful vest, and a plain blouse or shirt. Instructions for wrapping the towel turban:

  1. Use a thin, lightweight bath towel or long dishtowel; it should be light enough to stay on your head throughout the program and to wrap easily.

  2. Lean forward, dropping your head forward.

  3. Place the center of the long side of towel above the nape of your neck.

  4. Gather the short ends that are hanging down and twist them around each other.

  5. Stand up and tuck the ends into the back of the towel, above the nape of your neck. (Hint: This is done the same way wet hair is wrapped after washing.)

  6. Attach a large decorative pin to the front of the towel above your forehead.

Before You Begin

- Make a copy of the "StoryTrip to India Vocabulary List" handout for each child.

- Gather the equipment and materials.

- Review all materials and practice the program.

- Assemble and put on your genie costume.

Program

Introduction

> [Wear your genie costume.] Welcome to a "StoryTrip to India." We are going to glide on a magic carpet to visit an aging Bengal tiger in the jungles of India. You will have the opportunity to be the characters in the story. Then I, the Genie, will grant you three wishes and show you how to pose as a tiger! But first let's learn a bit about India.

Browse books on India with the children and show the location of India on the globe or world map. Give them the "StoryTrip to India Vocabulary List." Go over the words and their pronunciation. Have the children repeat the words. Browse the nonfiction books on the Bengal tiger.

Story Presentation (5–10 Minutes)

Leader: *As you now know, the Bengal tiger is an endangered species. Most of these tigers that are not in zoos around the world live in the jungles of India. A hundred years ago there were 100,000 Bengal tigers; today there are fewer than 5,000. There are so few because people have destroyed their homes, the forests and grasslands, and killed them for their bones, skins, teeth, and nails. We've even made rugs out of them!*

[Tell or read *The Tiger Skin Rug*. I have given the Tiger a name: Rags.]

Story Vocal and Movement Exercises

Part 1: Magic Carpet Ride (10 Minutes)

Leader: *And now, I will unfurl my magic carpet.* [Spread out the "magic carpet" and have children sit on it.]

Welcome to the Magic CarPort. As your Genie, I will be your "Guide for the Glide." You have boarded the magic carpet for the ride of a lifetime. To the stars and then to India we shall go. You will see many things along the way. [Have the children stand up; they should stand arm's distance from the person to the side, in front of, and behind them. Children should imitate the following movements:]

1. Leader: *We're gliding up into the sky*

Movement: With your palms down, raise your arms in front of you, reaching up diagonally.

2. Leader: *Higher and higher, we go*

Movement: With your palms down, undulate your arms, dipping them down slightly and then up, higher each time (three times).

3. Leader: *We are gliding to the right.*

Movement: With your palms down, stretch your arms out at chest level and twist gently and slowly to the right.

4. Leader: *We are gliding to the left.*

Movement: With your palms down, stretch your arms out at chest level and twist gently and slowly to the left.

5. Leader: *Sailing smoothly*

Movement: Sit down and have the children sit down on the magic carpet.

6. Leader: *We are gaining altitude.* [Say and demonstrate the following:] *Inhale deeply and exhale slowly. Breath in the fresh air. Inhale deeply and exhale slowly, and as you exhale, say "ahhhh" very slowly, two times. Close your eyes and imagine what you might see below and around you. Keep your eyes closed as you listen to this song; listen to the words.* [Wait a few moments in silence and then play the "Magic Carpet Ride."]

Open your eyes slowly, look around, and imagine now that you are sitting among the stars. Let us dance among the stars. [Ask the children one by one to get up and tell and dance what they saw (visualized when their eyes were closed). Have them speak about and dance about what they saw around the magic carpet. As they speak and dance, have them go around the entire carpet before returning to their seats. If they run out of images, have them repeat what they said and did until they reach their seats.]

Part 2: Story Scenes (15 Minutes)

Review the characters' names or titles and have the children volunteer to be one of the characters in the story. If you used another story, change the characters and the character sketches. To give everyone a turn, have one set of children at a time be the characters in the following scenes. Repeat the sequence of scenes for each set of children.

Leader: *Now you have the opportunity to make up words and movement for each of the following scenes:*

1. Scene One: Introduction of Characters: Tiger, Rajah, Children, Wives, Burglars, Servant who cleans the rugs. [Have each character get up in front of the group and say something about who he or she is and make a few movements or poses to depict the character's looks and personality.]

2. Scene Two: Rags pretends to be a rug.

The servant beats the rugs over the clothesline, including Rags, the tiger, who is acting as a rug.

Rags lies on the floor as the family has dinner.

The family leaves and Rags eats all the leftovers.

The children and the Rajah pretend the rug is real and play games with it. The tiger skin rug does not move by itself; it is moved about by the children.

3. Scene Three: Rags gains weight.

The Rajah notices that the rug is looking healthier and fatter.

The Rajah has the servant hang Rags outside over the clothesline and clean Rags (the rug) thoroughly because he is beginning to smell.

4. Scene Four: Rags saves the Rajah.

The burglars steel expensive serving dishes and jewelry.

The Rajah discovers the burglars and they try to attack him.

Rags roars and chases off the burglars.

The burglars all get stuck in the window together, trying to escape.

5. Scene Five: Rags gets his wish.

Rags is now one of the family. He goes on picnics with them, swims in their pool, and rides on elephants.

The children play with him.

The wives adore him.

Rags is happy!

Part 3: Make-a-Wish Charade (15 Minutes)

Leader: *What did the tiger wish for? His wish came true; I granted him that wish. Now I'm going to grant you three wishes; I will tell you about them one at a time.* [Give the children time to close their eyes and imagine their wishes.]

1. Wish Number 1—Something Delicious to Eat

Leader: *Your first wish is for something delicious that you love to eat or maybe never have eaten yet. Close your eyes and imagine eating that food.* [Have several children, one at a time, dance their food wishes, making their movements larger than life, for example, exaggerate by using all parts of their bodies to express the eating, the exuberance, and the shape of the food. The rest of the group should guess what the dancer is eating.]

2. Wish Number 2—Something You'd Like to Wear

Leader: *Your second wish is for something that you would like to wear. Close your eyes and imagine that you are putting it on and then modeling it, showing off its special features. Now you are going to do it through movement.* [Have several children, one at a time; dance their clothing wishes, making exaggerated movements. The rest of the group should guess what clothing they are wearing and modeling.]

3. Wish Number 3—A Place That You Would Like to Visit and What You Would Do There.

Leader: *Your third and last wish is a place to which you like to go and do something. Close your eyes and imagine that you are there and doing something special. Now do it through movement.* [Have several children, one at a time, dance their dream places and activities, making exaggerated movements. The rest of the group should guess where they are and what they are doing.]

Part 4: Magic Carpet Yoga (5 Minutes)

On the magic carpet, teach the children the "Yoga Tiger Pose."

Leader:

1. *Pretend that you are a tiger on all fours (two palms and two knees); with your palms on the floor and a slight bend in your elbows, bend your knees so that they touch the ground beneath your hips. Begin with a flat back.*

2. *Take a big breath and arch your back, dropping your head toward your chest.*

3. *Bring your right knee toward your chest and see if you can touch your knee to your forehead.*

4. *Let out a big breath and drop your tummy a bit, then look up to the ceiling and gently extend your right leg back, with your knee bent and your foot pointed toward the ceiling.*

5. *Now do the same thing with your left leg.*

6. *Sit back on your hips and gently drop your forehead to the floor, letting your arms rest on the floor by your legs.*

7. *Slowly roll up your back, one vertebra at a time, with your head the last thing to uncurl.*

StoryTrip to India Vocabulary List

Altitude. A high location above sea level.

Imagine. To see something in your mind, creating a mental picture. (Demonstrate this by closing your eyes and saying something like: "a tree in blossom" or "a mermaid lounging on a rock by the sea".)

Endangered Species. A species whose numbers are so small that it is at risk of extinction.

Extinct. No longer in existence, all gone.

Rajah or Raja. A prince, chief, or ruler in India or the East Indies.

StoryTrip to India Vocabulary List

Altitude. A high location above sea level.

Imagine. To see something in your mind, creating a mental picture. (Demonstrate this by closing your eyes and saying something like: "a tree in blossom" or "a mermaid lounging on a rock by the sea".)

Endangered Species. A species whose numbers are so small that it is at risk of extinction.

Extinct. No longer in existence, all gone.

Rajah or Raja. A prince, chief, or ruler in India or the East Indies.

From *Stories on the Move: Integrating Literature and Movement with Children, Infants to Age 14* by Arlene Cohen. Illustrated by Andrea Fitcha McAllister. Westport, CT: Libraries Unlimited. Copyright © 2007.

Program 4: StoryTrip to Japan

Summary

After hearing the story, "The Old Man with a Wen," the children board and become the plane for a flight to Japan. They learn the character voices and improvise dances at the Haunted Dojo. They have an opportunity to brainstorm an alternative plot and reenact the story or alternative plot in the Goblin's Forest. The children visit the Kabuki Theater and learn some traditional Onnegata (female) dance steps and vocabulary. They make fans before they visit the Kabuki Theater. This program takes between 60 and 90 minutes, including the introduction. The last half hour is for making fans and doing the Kabuki dance.

Program Preparation

Books

- Bang, Molly, selector. "The Old Man with a Wen." In *The Goblins Giggle and Other Stories*. Illustrated by Molly Bang. Gloucester, MA: P. Smith, 1988, 1973. An old man, with an unsightly and bothersome bump on his face, takes a walk into the forest and ends up dancing with goblins. To make sure that he comes back to dance with them again, they steal his only mark of beauty, his bump.

- Sakade, Florence, comp. *Japanese Children's Favorite Stories: Book Two*. Illustrated by Yoshio Hasaki. Boston: C. E. Tuttle, 2004. Has a shorter version of the story.

Books on Japan

- Heinrichs, Ann. *Japan.* New York: Children's Press, 2006.

- Rex, Shelley, Teo Chuu Yong, and Russell Mok. *Japan.* New York: Marshall Cavendish, 2002.

- Temko, Florence. *Traditional Crafts from Japan*. Illustrated by Randall Gooch. Minneapolis, MN: Lerner Publications, 2001.

Books and Web Sites on Kabuki Theater

- Brandon, James R., and Samuel L. Leiter, eds. *Kabuki Plays on Stage*. Honolulu: University of Hawaii Press, 2002.

- Cavaye, Ronald. *Kabuki: A Pocket Guide*. Photographs by Tomoko Ogawa. Ruthland, VT: C. E. Tuttle, 1993.

- Spencer, Michael. *Kabuki Story 2001/Anatomy of Kabuki: Costume*. 1999. Kabuki costumes may be viewed at http://www.lightbrigade.demon.co.uk/Breakdown/Costume.htm.

- Nishikawa Masaki performing a segment of a traditional Japanese dance. A Kabuki Onnegata Dance can be viewed at http://www.amphi.com/~psteffen/fmf/kabuki3.html.

- Japanese instruments can be viewed at the following sites:

  - Déry, Bernard. *InfoVisual.Info, Volume 4. Japanese Instruments, 2005–2006.* http://www.infovisual.info/04/007_en.html.

  - "Japanese Instruments." In *Wikipedia: The Free Encyclopedia.* Wikimedia Foundation Inc., 2006. http://en.wikipedia.org/wiki/Category:Japanese_instruments.

Music

- Alternative lullaby source: Walty, Margaret. *Rock-a-Bye Baby: Lullabies for Bedtime.* Brooklyn, NY: Barefoot Books, 1998, 1997.

- Ensemble Nipponia. "Ataka no Matsui," from *Japan: Kabuki & Other Traditional Music.* New York: Nonesuch, [1995].

- Kidz Bop Kids. "Haunted House," from *Kidz Bop Halloween.* New York: Razor & Tie Direct, 2004.

- A march from one the following CDs:

  - *Meredith Willson's The Music Man.* Hollywood, CA: Capitol Records, [1983–1991].

  - *America the Beautiful Boston Pops Orchestra.* [Netherlands]: Philips; New York: Marketed by PolyGram Classics & Jazz, 1996.

  - *The Enchanted Carousal [i.e. Carousel]: Old Fashioned Band Organ Music.* North Hollywood, CA: Klavier, 1990.

- "Run-up Engines, Taxi," "Take-off into Constant Flight," "Land, Taxi to Halt," and other airplane warm up sounds, from *Transport.* Princeton, NJ: Films for the Humanities & Sciences, [1991], 1986.

- "Tree Spirit" and "Japanese Lullaby," from *Floating Clouds.* Portland, OR: Moonbridge, 1995.

Space Needs

- Open, uncarpeted movement space, about 2 to 3 square feet per child

- Tables and chairs for coloring and folding fans

Materials and Equipment

- CD and cassette player

- Prerecorded cassette tape of dialogue (see below).

- Percussion instrument (e.g., flat hand drum and drum stick or sealed oatmeal box and wooden spoon)

- Globe or world map

- Handouts: "StoryTrip to Japan Vocabulary List" and "Character Dialogue," one for each child (at end of this chapter)

- Paper fan materials: crayons, 8½-by-11-inch, 20-lb. paper, scotch tape

- Pictures from Web searches or books on Kabuki showing zori, kimono, koto, hanamichi, and performers.

Before You Begin

- Make copies of the "Character Dialogue" and "StoryTrip to Japan Kabuki Theater Vocabulary List" handouts for each child.

- Gather all materials and equipment.

- Review the program and practice the Onnegata Dance.

- Make a sample fan.

- Record the character voices listed on the handout on a blank cassette tape, leaving pause time for the children to repeat the dialogue and make up the movement. Speak the voices in an eerie, strange manner. The dialogue will take place in the "Haunted Dojo."

- Print out pictures of Kabuki from a Web site or have Kabuki books to show pictures.

Program

Introduction

> [Play airplane warm up sounds in the piece, "Run-up Engines, Taxi."] Welcome, children to the airport. After we hear a story today, we will board an airplane and fly the Plane of Imagination, across the sky, for a "StoryTrip to Japan." There we will visit the Haunted Dojo, the Goblin Forest, and a Kabuki Theater. You are going to have the opportunity to be storytellers today.

Browse books on Japan with the children and show the location of Japan on the globe or world map.

Story Presentation

Read or tell "The Old Man with a Wen."

Story Vocal and Movement Exercises

Part 1: The Plane of Imagination (10 Minutes)

Line children up in four rows to move from one side of the room to the other.

Leader: *Now we going to board and become the plane of imagination. Please remain upright; in other words, please don't fall on the floor or go completely to the ground on all fours; do change levels: high, medium, and low when the instruction suggests that. Feel free to add plane sounds to your movement, too.*

Have the children move one length of the room for each image, except for the first one, during which they remain still and warm up their engines. They can make whatever sounds or movement with their arms and legs they want, as long as they are moving forward and changing levels, as implied by each image. Use the drum as noted, to give the feeling of each movement. Repeat each drum motion until children are on the other side of the room. For the first image, repeat the drum circles several times, until you sense the children are done "warming up" the plane engine.

In the background play "Run-up Engines, Taxi" for instruction 1; "Take-off into Constant Flight" for instructions 2–8; and "Land, Taxi to Halt" for instructions 9–10. A second person to play the CD or the drum or call out the movement instructions would be helpful here. If you don't have a second person, it is suggested that you do just the drumming or just the CD.

Demonstrate the levels: low or bent knees (L); middle or regular height (M); high or reaching and up on the balls of feet (H).

1. **Leader:** *The Plane is warming up, rev up your engines, low level with bent knees (L).*

   Drum: Lightly make circles on the drum surface with the drumstick.

2. **Leader:** *Wheels leaving the ground, reach up high, stretch (H). Begin to move forward.*

   Drum: Make progressively faster beats, accelerando.

3. **Leader:** *Rising up into the air, high and light and lighter and higher and lighter (H)*

   Drum: Make steadily lighter and lighter beats.

4. **Leader:** *Smooth flying; you are gliding smoothly (M).*

   Drum: Run the drumstick slowly back and forth over the drum.

5. **Leader:** *There is turbulence (L), (M), (H), and repeat a few times, changing levels.*

   Drum: Make quick and sharp beats.

6. **Leader:** *Smooth, Bumpy, Smooth*

   Drum: Run the drumstick slowly back and forth and then alternate with quick and sharp beats.

7. **Leader:** *Curving to the right, curving to the left*

   Drum: Make one sharp beat for each curve.

8. Leader: *Smooth flying (M)*

Drum: Run the drumstick slowly back and forth.

9. Leader: *Slowly descending (L)*

Drum: Make progressively slower beats, deccelerando.

10. Leader: *You are getting ready to land; your wheels have dropped.*

Drum: Make two simultaneous beats, then pause for two counts and repeat.

11. Leader: *We have landed and at the Haunted Dojo in Japan; we will meet the Old Man and Goblins inside.*

Part 2: The Haunted Dojo (15 Minutes)

Play the following as background music, while you arrange children in the room: "Tree Spirit" or "Haunted House."

Leader: *It is the custom in Japan to remove your shoes outside the entrance to the Dojo, place your palms together, as if in prayer, and bow deeply from the waist as you enter the Dojo. Bowing is a sign of respect; this is a sacred place.*

Divide the class in half. One half will be Old Men and the other half will be the Goblins. Seat the Old Men on one side of the movement space and the Goblins on the other side. Give them the "StoryTrip to Japan Character Dialogue" handout and play the prerecorded tape. Have them practice all of their dialogue before they do the movement and then have them say the dialogue with the movement. Pause the tape when they are doing the movement. Refer to the written dialogue to keep the improvisation going.

Leader: *The Old Men will speak and improvise dances to the following*:

Old Men (OM): I love to dance, do youuuuuuu? I can dance to marches; can youuuuuuuu? Can you dance to this one?

Play a march. Have the Old Men walk four counts or steps in one direction and then change direction every four counts. Encourage them to go in different directions than the others. This is not a follow-the-leader dance; it is an individual direction and space dance. They need to look ahead and avoid bumping into others.

OM: That was very good; I can dance to lullabies; can youuuuuuuu? Can you dance to this one?

Play a lullaby and have them rock and turn around the room, watching out to not bump into others. They will rock and whirl around others.

OM: I can dance when there is no music at all; can youuuuuu? Let's see you dance now.

Don't play any music. Encourage the children to just make up anything.

Leader: *Now the goblins will speak and dance in the following sequence:*

Goblins (G): I dance to silly songs; can youuuuuu? Here's a silly song; can you dance to it? I'll sing and you dance.

G: Dough, dough, dough, dough

G: Shriek, shriek, shriek, shriek

G: Cluck, Cluck

G: Clack, Clack

G: Shriekkkkkkkkkkkkkkkkkkkkkkk!

Leader: *Now the Old Men and the Goblins dance together:*

OM: That was great! I'll dance with you this time.

OM & G: Dough, dough, dough, dough

OM & G: Shriek, shriek, shriek, shriek

OM & G: Cluck, Cluck

OM & G: Clack, Clack

OM & G: Shriekkkkkkkkkkkkkkkkkkkkkkk!

G: Old Man, do you know the "Count Down Song"? It goes like this:

G: 8,7, 6, 5, 4, 3, 2

G: 8,7, 6, 5, 4, 3, 2

OM: You forgot "1."

G & OM: Let's all dance to the "Count Down Song."

G: 8,7, 6, 5, 4, 3, 2

G: 8,7, 6, 5, 4, 3, 2

OM: "1."

Part 3: What If . . . (10 Minutes)

Leader: *I am going to ask you some questions about the events in the story, the plot. When you give your answer, I want you to stand up and project your voice across the room, so everyone can hear you.* [Ask the following plot questions:]

1. Leader: *What would have happened if the Goblins hadn't let the Old Man leave?*

2. Leader: *What would the Goblins say and do to get him to stay?*

3. Leader: *What would the Old Man have said and done then?*

4. Leader: *What would happen next?* [Repeat this question as long as there are answers coming from the children or until you feel it's time to move on to the ending.]

5. Leader: *How does your story end?*

6. Leader: *Does anyone else have another ending?* [Repeat this question as long as there are answers coming from the children or until you feel it's time to finish.]

Part 4: The Kabuki Theater (15 Minutes)

Leader: *Now we are going to visit a theater in Japan; it is called the Kabuki Theater. Kabuki theater is very entertaining; it is a dance with a story and music.*

Give children the "StoryTrip to Japan Kabuki Theater Vocabulary List" handout. Review the terms from the vocabulary list and have the children pronounce them as transliterated.

Show the children the books, pictures, or Web sites depicting costumes, instruments, and a dance.

Have the children color and fold fans:

- Color any pattern or picture on the paper.

- Accordion pleat the paper from the horizontal side, with folds measuring about 1 inch apart.

- Gather pleats at the bottom 2 inches and wrap tape around them.

Create a meditative mood:

- To center everyone in a meditative mood, have them inhale and then slowly exhale three times.

- Gently press the palm of your hand on your diaphragm between the ribs to exhale slowly and completely.

Teach the children the following Onnegata-type dance movements, before putting on the music, "Ataka no Matsui."

Leader:

> *Line up single file, holding your fans in the open position with the decorated side facing out. Hold your fans just above your waist, close to your chest.*

> *Imagine that you are walking down the hanamichi, the center walkway from the main stage. You are wearing a colorful kimono and zori on your feet.*

> *Your knees are slightly bent. Your feet are turned inward.*

> *Slowly slide your right foot just in front of your left foot. Take small steps, alternating right and left, sliding with a turned-in foot. Always move forward very slowly.*

> *Turn around and continue the walk in the other direction.*

> *Every once and a while, stop walking and position your arms: one arm going up, bent or straight, one sideways bent or straight. Your arms can change, but they should be set in place deliberately, as if posed, each time you stop. Once your arms and body are posed, tilt your head slowly and gently to the side; your face must always be facing front as you tilt it, with a serious expression.*

End with a bow by putting first one knee down on the floor and then the other, and sitting back on your heels, placing your fan on floor about a foot in front of your knees and placing your palms on the floor in front of your knees, dropping your back and your head forward in a bowing motion.

Now let's do the dance with the music.

Part 5: Flying Home (5 Minutes)

Return home on the plane of imagination. The children can improvise.

StoryTrip to Japan Kabuki Theater Vocabulary List (Transliterated)

Dojo (dough joe). A school for training in the Japanese arts of self-defense, such as judo and karate. It also is a place to practice meditation.

Hanamichi (Hannah me chee). Central walkway that is an extension of the Kabuki stage

Kabuki (ka boo key). A type of popular Japanese drama in which elaborately costumed performers, men only, use stylized movements, dances, and songs to enact tragedies and comedies. The story is chanted by a narrator.

Onnagata (o na ga ta). A female role played by a male. All roles are played by men in Kabuki.

Clothing Worn by Kabuki Performers

Kimono (key moan o). An elaborate robe.

Zori (zor ee). Straw sandals.

Instruments in the Kabuki Ensemble

Koto (co toe). A stringed instrument held in the lap and plucked; resembles a zither.

Shakuhacki (sha coo hach ee). A bamboo flute.

Shamisen (sha me san). A Japanese musical instrument resembling a lute, having a very long neck and three strings, played with a plectrum.

Taiko (tie co). A Japanese drum.

StoryTrip to Japan Character Dialogue

Leader: *Old Men will speak and improvise dances to the following:*

    Old Men (OM): I love to dance, do youuuuuu?

    OM: I can dance to marches; can youuuuuuuu? Can you dance to this one?

    OM: That was very good; I can dance to lullabies; can youuuuuuuu? Can you dance to this one?

    OM: I can dance when there is no music at all; can youuuuuu? Let's see you dance now.

Leader: *Now the goblins will speak and dance in the following sequence:*

    Goblins (G): I dance to silly songs; can youuuuuu? Here's a silly song; can you dance to it? I'll sing and you dance.

    G: Dough, dough, dough, dough

    G: Shriek, shriek, shriek, shriek

    G: Cluck, Cluck, Clack, Clack

    G: Shriekkkkkkkkkkkkkkkkkkkkkkkk!

Leader: *Now the Old Man and the Goblins dance together:*

    OM: That was great! I'll dance with you this time.

    OM & G: Dough, dough, dough, dough

    OM & G: Shriek, shriek, shriek, shriek

    OM & G: Cluck, Cluck

    OM & G: Clack, Clack

    OM & G: Shriekkkkkkkkkkkkkkkkkkkkkkkk!

    G: Old Man, do you know the "Count Down Song"? It goes like this:

    G: 8,7, 6, 5, 4, 3, 2

    G: 8,7, 6, 5, 4, 3, 2

    OM: You forgot "1."

    G & OM: Let's all dance to the "Count Down Song."

    G: 8,7, 6, 5, 4, 3, 2

    G: 8,7, 6, 5, 4, 3, 2

    OM: "1."

Chapter 5

StoryImage: Ages Nine to Eleven

Introduction

The Hawaiian StoryImage™ programs teach children how to creatively interpret story structure and the story elements of setting, character, plot, and narration. All the activities in the Hawaiian StoryImage programs revolve around the well-known Hawaiian myth, "Ohia and Lehua." It is one of the stories in *The Goddess Pele* by Joe Mullins. Every library in Hawaii has several copies, and it is available elsewhere through interlibrary loan. The first two programs can be done independently; the third requires having done one of the first two programs. Through guided vocal and movement warm-ups and improvisation, children learn how to infuse shapes with moods to convey setting, character, and event images. In each part they perform an animated image for the rest of the children in the group. As they speak and move, it is like seeing still pictures come to life! The still picture or posed shape becomes a moving image using the dynamics of size and mood. Shape collages and visualizations help them to conceive the shapes that they will be performing. They can use their shape collages as they practice and tell their story passages. They make up new dialogue based on narration that describes characters.

If you do not have a background in storytelling and wish to perform the literature, see the "Trigger Method of Learning a Story (Group Leader)" handout at the end of chapter 6.

In the poetry StoryImage program children have the opportunity to memorize and perform a short poem. As in the Hawaiian StoryImage, the goal is to animate the images to bring them to life.

Vocal expressiveness replaces recorded music in these programs.

The final program, "Mirrors of Trees" StoryImage, is composed of several parts that can be done consecutively or separately. The children write, draw, and make up movements to mirror the growth cycle of a tree in a variety of formations: as a one-person tree, as a grove, and as a composite tree formed by the group.

Details about 9- to 11-year-olds' cognitive and physical skills are outlined in Table 5.1.

Table 5.1. Readiness to Learn (9- to 11-Year-Olds)

COGNITIVE	PHYSICAL
➢ Beginnings of abstract thought ➢ Problem solving ➢ Social speech ➢ Creative interpretation of story imagery ➢ Awareness of moods and emotions ➢ Ability to memorize passages	➢ Ability to create a series of movements and repeat them ➢ Awareness and creative use of personal space for movement ➢ Ability to create body shapes ➢ Interpretive movement based on mood

Program 1: Hawaiian StoryImage— Setting Interpretation

Summary

In Program 1 the children hear the "Ohia and Lehua" story and identify the sequence of events, characters, and settings. Then they select, visualize, and interpret one story setting using voice and motion. They become animated shapes of the objects in the settings. They perform the settings in sequence for the other children in the group. Program 1 lasts about two and a half hours, including the introduction.

Program Preparation

Books

• Mullins, Joe. "Ohia and Lehua." In *The Goddess Pele*. Honolulu: Aloha Graphics, 1977. Disguised as a beautiful young woman, the Fire Goddess Pele tempts Chief Ohia to marry her and takes her revenge when he refuses.

Other Sources of Pele Stories

• Kanahele, Pualani Kanaka'ole. *Holo Mai Pele*. Translated by Ku'ulei Higashi. Edited by D. Mahealani Dudoit. Honolulu: Pacific Islanders in Communications; Hilo, Hawaii: Edith Kanaka'ole Foundation, 2001. Documented performance of a dramatic epic of Pele, with excellent photographs and text of the performance.

• Nordenstrom, Michael. *Pele and the Rivers of Fire*. Honolulu: Bess Press, 2002.

• Verniero, Joan C., and Robin Fitzsimmons, eds. *An Illustrated Treasury of Read-Aloud Myths and Legends: The World's Best-Loved Myths and Legends for Parent and Child to Share*. New York: Black Dog & Leventhal Publishers, distributed by Workman Publishing, 2004.

• Wichman, Frederick B. *Pele Ma: Legends of Pele from Kaua'i.* Honolulu: Bamboo Ridge Press, 2001. Contains three stories about Pele and Lohi'au, a chief from Kauai. There are similarities to the "Ohia and Lehua" story in these stories.

Also of Interest

• *Hawaiian Word Book.* Illustrated by Robin Yoko Burningham, with a foreword by Lokomaika`iokalani Snakenberg. Honolulu: Bess Press, c1983. Line drawings illustrate simple Hawaiian words such as *keiki, halakahiki,* and *Pele,* grouped together in categories such as Hawaiian life style, the body, and nature. Includes Hawaiian and English glossaries.

Music

• The Brothers Kanilau. "E Pele, E Pele" or "Aia la'O Pele I Hawai'i" chant, from *Mele Oli: Chants from Ancient Hawai'i.* Boulder, CO: Sounds True, 1998.

• The Makaha Sons (Moon, John & Jerome) & Friends. *Na pua o Hawaiì.* Honolulu: Poki, 2001.

• *Pride of Punahele II.* [Hawaii]: Punahele Productions, 2003.

Space Needs

• Open space, about 2 to 3 square feet per child. Floor should be smooth: tiled or wood.

• Tables or desks and chairs, or cushions on floor with clipboards on which to write, glue, and draw.

The environment should be free of interference noises such as those in a cafeteria.

Materials and Equipment

• CD and cassette player

• Large sheets of butcher paper (cut to approximately 17 by 22 inches)

• Masking tape

• Glue sticks or tape

• Pencils and crayons or colored pens

• Paper for writing what children see in their visualizations

• Cutouts of text of setting-related images from list below

• Handouts:

  – "Story Elements and Imagery" (at end of this section)

  – "Hawaiian StoryImage Vocabulary List (Transliterated)" (at end of this section; the list appears twice on the handout so you can cut the copy in half and provide for two children from each copy)

  – "Setting Images of the Ohia and Lehua Story" (at end of this section)

  – "Shapes" (at end of this section)

Before You Begin

- Rehearse or review the story.

- Gather all materials and equipment.

- Make copies of all handouts, one for each child. Make one enlarged copy (200 percent) of "Setting Images of the Ohia and Lehua Story" and cut out each image for children to glue or tape to the bottom of their collages.

- Cut two sets of setting images (works for 22 children; adjust the amount).

- Review the program and handout contents.

- Learn the transliterated Hawaiian vocabulary.

- Listen to the music.

Program

Introduction

> Welcome to the Hawaiian StoryImage workshop. After hearing a story about the fire Goddess Pele, each of you will select a setting image to interpret through voice and movement. Shape collages, visualization, and a vocal and movement warm-up will prepare you for your interpretations. First let's review the elements of a story. [Give children the "Story Elements and Imagery" handout and review the "Elements" section with them.] Stories have the following elements:
>
> **Plot.** The plot is the sequence of events in a story, that is, what happens first, second, third, and so on.
>
> **Characters.** Characters do the acting in a story.
>
> **Settings with objects.** Setting is where and when the story takes place. Today, when you hear the story, pay particular attention to where the story is taking place and the objects in the that setting.

Story Presentation (10 Minutes)

Leader: Mele *is sung poetry. I will play one about Pele, the Hawaiian Fire Goddess. Before and during the performance of an ancient hula in Hawaii, a* mele *is chanted. There are many* meles *and* mo'olelo *or stories for the Goddess Pele. When Pele gets angry, she becomes molten lava, erupting from the volcano and spewing down the side of the mountain toward the sea. Everything in her path is destroyed.*

Play one of the Pele selections to set the mood.

The Ohia and Lehua Story

Read or tell "Ohia and Lehua."

Story Vocal and Movement Exercises

Part 1: The Story Elements in Ohia and Lehua (10 Minutes)

Go over the elements of the story of Ohia and Lehua.

Leader: [Ask the children what they remember about the plot of the story and fill in the following where necessary:] *In Ohia and Lehua, first, Pele and Ohia meet; second, Pele proposes marriage; third, Ohia refuses; fourth, Pele takes revenge; fifth Lehua pleads for Ohia's life; and sixth, the Gods change Lehua into a blossom on the tree.*

[Ask the children who the characters are in the story and fill in the following where necessary.] *Who does the acting in this story? Ohia, Lehua, Pele, and the Gods.*

In Ohia and Lehua, several settings are portrayed. Can someone recall the various settings and objects in this story? [As before, affirm and complete the answers:] *In the woods, the sea, a twisted gnarled Ohia tree, the volcano Halemaumau, the Lehua blossoms on the tree.*

Part 2: Setting Image Selection, Visualization, and Collage (40 Minutes)

Leader: *Stories are composed of images that activate our imaginations.* [Draw the children's attention to the second section on their handout about images.] *There are images of the characters, the setting, and the plot. In our imagination we not only* **see** *images, we also* **hear, smell, feel, touch,** *and* **taste** *them—and we imagine how they move. I'd like you to choose one of the setting images to draw and perform. All setting images should be chosen.*

Give students a copy of the "Setting Images of Ohia and Lehua Story" handout and the "Hawaiian StoryImage Vocabulary List (Transliterated)" handout. Go over the pronunciation of the Hawaiian words as transliterated and the meanings and have the children repeat them a few times after you.

Have the students pick one of the images from the list and give them an enlarged copy of the text of the image that they have selected. First have the children read their setting image to themselves a couple of times. Then have them close their eyes and listen to what you say. Give them plenty of time between visualizations before going on to the next item.

Leader: *While keeping your eyes closed, I want you to imagine how your setting or object looks. . . . Now I want you to imagine how it might smell. . . . Now I want you to imagine how it might feel, if you touched it. . . . Now I want you to imagine how it might sound. . . . Now I want you to imagine how the objects in the setting might move.*

After the visualization, have them write how their setting looked in their visualization. Then distribute the copies of the "Shapes" handout (at end of this section) and have them cut out the shapes and create collages of the settings.

Have them draw details of the setting within the shapes that best fit the objects in the setting. They can recut once they have made the drawing *inside* the borders of the shape, as long as the basic shape is still obvious. Then have them arrange the shapes on the butcher paper and glue them to the paper. Have them leave space at the bottom of their pictures to glue on the enlarged text.

Part 3: Vocal and Movement Warm-up and Improvisation (45 Minutes)

Leader: *We are going to say each of the following vocal warm up sounds* **three** *times each.*

Inhale, exhale slowly, making the Ommmmmm sound

Inhale, exhale: Ma Me Mi Mo Mu

Inhale, exhale: Ta Te Ti To Tu

Inhale, exhale wolf yowl: Ah Ouuuuu

Inhale, exhale: NeNeNeNe

Inhale, exhale witch laugh: Ha! Ha! Ha! Ha! Ha!

Now we are going to make shapes—big ones, small ones, narrow ones, and wide ones—with the different parts of our body. But first we are going to create a kinesphere in which we will make these shapes. A kinesphere is like a bubble that we create around our bodies. You will stay in your bubble. Your bubble is your personal space, and you will be moving within your bubble **not** *across or around the room or touching others.*

My Kinesphere.

- *Raise your arms to the side at shoulder level, parallel to the floor. Move apart so that you don't touch anyone else.*

- *Make one one-quarter turn to the right and again raise your arms to the side at shoulder level, parallel to the floor. Again adjust your space so that you are not touching anyone.*

- *Make another one-quarter turn to your right (you are opposite to where you started). Raise your arms as before.*

- *Make another one-quarter turn to your right and raise your arms as before.*

- *Make a final one-quarter turn to your right, facing front, where you started.*

- *Gently do the following; do not strain: Roll your body down by dropping your head forward, then your shoulders; ease your knees by bending them slightly, then roll down the rest of your back. Reverse slowly: roll up your back, keeping your head dropping heavily forward, and roll up your shoulders, then uncurl your neck as you raise your head to its normal position.*

- *Make sure that you are not touching anyone as you create and complete your bubble.*

[Give children the following directions. Do not model these but rather let them create what they imagine. Remind them to stay in their bubbles; their movements should not touch others.]

- *Draw a triangle in space with the following body parts as I call them out: your head, your shoulders, your arms, your elbows, and your hands.*

- *With your whole body create a triangle. Make it a very small triangle. Expand your triangle, making a very large triangle. Repeat, making your whole body triangular, smaller and larger, two more times. Repeat, making your whole body triangular, smaller and larger, two more times. The transition between the two sizes is very important, as this is how we see the formation take place.*

- *Draw a square in space with the following body parts as I call them out: your head, your shoulders, your arms, your elbows, and your hands.*

- *With your whole body create a square. Make it a very small square. Expand your square, making a very large square. Repeat, making your whole body square-shaped, smaller and larger, two more times.*

- *Draw a circle in space with the following body parts as I call them out: your head, your shoulders, your arms, your elbows, your hands, and your hips.*

- *With your whole body create a circle. Make it a very small circle. Expand your circle, making a very large circle.*

- *Draw an object from your selected setting image with your hand in the air and then step into the imaginary drawing, taking the shape of the object that you have drawn in the air. Narrow and widen the shape. Again the transition between narrow and wide or large and small is very important, as this is how we see the object or setting form in front of our eyes.*

- *Instead of drawing it first, take the shape right away; become the shape, pause, and pose in that shape for a couple of moments. Once you have the correct size and form, move however that object moves. For example, if it is a tree that becomes twisted and gnarled, move with a twist and a gnarl.*

- *Take the shape and movement again, applying a mood to it; do the shape with feeling or a mood, such as happy, sad, peaceful, angry, or afraid.*

- *Memorize the text of your image, then glue the text to the bottom of your drawing and combine your movement with your spoken text. Use a happy, sad, angry, or frightened voice to match your movement. Work within a 2- to 3-foot-square space.*

Part 4: Presentations (40 Minutes)

Use the masking tape to tape the drawings in sequence, one on top of the other, on an easel or on the wall as a storyboard. If you have 22 children, there will be two sets of drawings and two rounds of performances. Have children perform for the rest of the group their setting images as rehearsed, taking the small shape and then animating by moving into the large shape and then moving as the object moves, using their selected mood, in the sequence in which the images appear in the story. If they need to refer to the text, it will be visible at the bottom of their pictures.

Shapes

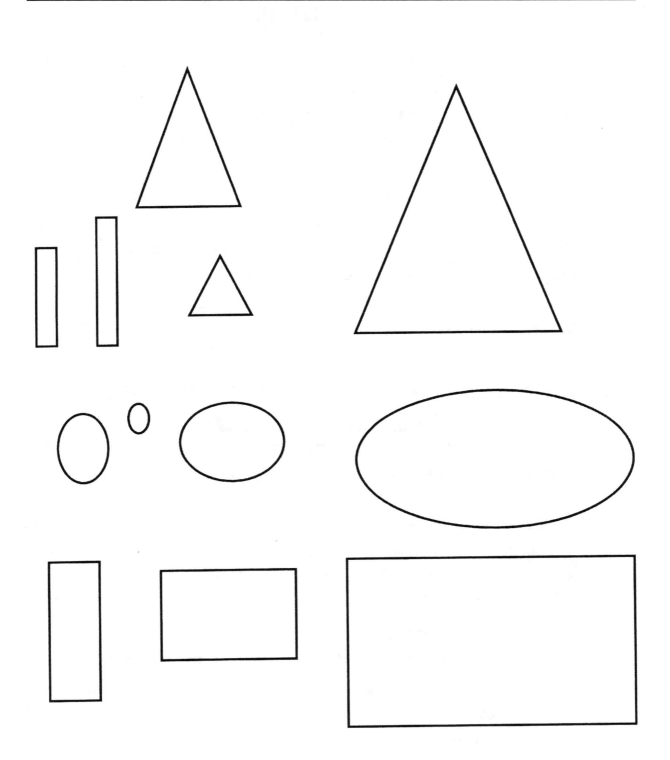

Hawaiian StoryImage Vocabulary List (Transliterated)

Halemaumau (Ha lay maow maow). A volcano on the Big Island of Hawaii.

Holua (ho lu a). A sled used on mud banks.

Kahiko (ka hee co). The ancient form of Hula.

Kileaua (kill a way a). A volcano on the Big Island of Hawaii.

Kukui (coo Coo e). A type of Hawaiian tree.

Ohia (o hee a). A chief of Kauai in this story; also a tree in Hawaii.

Pali (pa lee). A steep mountain pass.

Pele (pay lay). A Hawaiian fire goddess; also lava that flows out of the volcano.

Lehua (lay who a). The girlfriend of Ohia in this story; a blossom on the Ohia tree.

Mele (may lay). A poem that is chanted.

Mo'olelo (mo o lay lo). A prose narrative or story.

Hawaiian StoryImage Vocabulary List (Transliterated)

Halemaumau (Ha lay maow maow). A volcano on the Big Island of Hawaii.

Holua (ho lu a). A sled used on mud banks.

Kahiko (ka hee co). The ancient form of Hula.

Kileaua (kill a way a). A volcano on the Big Island of Hawaii.

Kukui (coo Coo e). A type of Hawaiian tree.

Ohia (o hee a). A chief of Kauai in this story; also a tree in Hawaii.

Pali (pa lee). A steep mountain pass.

Pele (pay lay). A Hawaiian fire goddess; also lava that flows out of the volcano.

Lehua (lay who a). The girlfriend of Ohia in this story; a blossom on the Ohia tree.

Mele (may lay). A poem that is chanted.

Mo'olelo (mo o lay lo). A prose narrative or story.

From *Stories on the Move: Integrating Literature and Movement with Children, Infants to Age 14* by Arlene Cohen. Illustrated by Andrea Fitcha McAllister. Westport, CT: Libraries Unlimited. Copyright © 2007.

Setting Images of the Ohia and Lehua Story

1. Kukui nut trees grow on the top of Mount Kilauea.

2. The bark from the Kukui Nut Tree is good for staining surfboards.

3. Mount Kilauea has been an active volcano for the last 20 years.

4. Depending on Pele's mood, the sea can be smooth, or have gentle waves that wash around the rocks.

5. Depending on Pele's mood, the surf can curl or thunder.

6. Depending on Pele's mood, the surf can shake the islands, or even cause a tidal wave that destroys land and people.

7. The Ohia tree is gnarled and ugly with gray-green leaves.

8. Near the Ohia tree, the cracked earth steamed with sulphur.

9. Halemaumau is a fuming and erupting volcano when Pele is angry.

10. The Ohia tree has beautiful red Lehua blossoms.

11. When the Lehua blossoms are picked, the rain falls; the rain is the tears of lost lovers.

Story Elements and Imagery

Elements

Plot. The sequence of events in a story, that is, what happens first, second, third, and so on.

Characters. Who does the acting in a story.

Settings with objects. Where and when the story takes place, and objects in the setting.

Literary Images

Stories are composed of images that activate our imagination. There are images of the characters, the setting, and the plot. In our imagination we not only see images, we also hear them, smell them, feel them, touch them, and taste them—and we imagine how they move.

Image Visualization

Close your eyes and imagine how your image

Looks

Smells

Feels inside (for characters and narrator)

Feels when you touch it (for objects and settings)

Tastes

Sounds

Program 2: Hawaiian StoryImage —Character Interpretation

Summary

In Program 2 the children hear and review the "Ohia and Lehua" story and identify the sequence of events, the characters, and the settings. If they have done Program 1 first, this will be a refresher. Then they select, visualize, and interpret one character image using voice and motion. They create dialogue for the character. They become the character in a part of the story, speaking and moving in character. They perform the character image in sequence for the other children in the group. Program 2 lasts about three hours, including the introduction.

Program Preparation

Books

Use the same list as in Program 1.

Space Needs

- Open space, about 2 to 3 square feet per child. Floor should be smooth: tiled or wood.
- Tables or desks and chairs, or cushions on floor with clipboards on which to write, paste, and draw.
- The environment should be free of interference noises such as those in a cafeteria.

Materials and Equipment

- CD and cassette player
- Pencils and crayons or colored pens
- Paper for writing what children see in their visualizations
- Handouts:
    - "Hawaiian StoryImage Vocabulary List (Transliterated)" (at end of Program 1), if needed
    - "Story Elements and Imagery" (at end of Program 1), if needed
    - "Ohia and Lehua Story Character Images" (at end of this section)
    - "Character Analysis Worksheet" (at end of this scetion)
    - "Shapes" (at end of Program 1)

Before You Begin

- Rehearse or review the story.
- Gather all materials and equipment.

- Make copies of all handouts, one for each child.

- Review the program and handouts.

- Learn the transliterated Hawaiian vocabulary.

- Listen to the music.

Program

Introduction

Welcome to the "Hawaiian StoryImage" workshop. After hearing a story about the Fire Goddess Pele, each of you will select a character image to interpret through voice and movement. Creating collages of shapes, visualization, and a vocal and movement warm-up will prepare you for your interpretations.

Story Presentation (10 Minutes)

Leader: Mele *is sung poetry. I will play one about Pele, the Hawaiian Fire Goddess. Before and during the performance of an ancient hula (*kahiko*)in Hawaii, a* mele *is chanted. There are many* meles *and* mo'olelo *or stories for the Goddess Pele. When Pele gets angry, she becomes molten lava, erupting from the volcano and spewing down the side of the mountain toward the sea. Everything in her path is destroyed.*

Play one of the Pele selections to set the mood.

The Ohia and Lehua Story

Read or tell "Ohia and Lehua."

Story Vocal and Movement Exercises

Part 1: The Story Elements in Ohia and Lehua (Review) (5 Minutes)

Leader: *First let's review the elements of a story.* [Give children the "Story Elements and Imagery" handout and review the "Elements" section with them.]

Ask questions, wait for answers, and then affirm with the answer. This is a review if you have done Program 1. If they don't already have a copy, give each child the "Story Elements and Imagery" handout.

Leader: *Stories are composed of literary elements. What are three story elements?*

Answer: Plot, Character, and Setting

Leader: *Would someone like to define* plot?

Answer: *Plot* is the sequence of events in a story, that is, what happens first, second, third and so on.

Leader: *Would someone define a* story setting?

Answer: Where and when the story takes place. Also, objects are part of the setting.

Leader: *Would someone like to define what story* characters *do?*

Answer: The characters act out the story.

Leader: *Who are the* characters *in Ohia and Lehua?*

Answer: Ohia, Lehua, Pele, the Bird Catchers, and the Gods.

Leader: *What are story* images?

Answer: Stories are composed of *images* that activate our imagination. There are images of the characters, the setting, and the plot. In our imagination we not only see images, we also hear them, smell them, feel them, touch them, and taste them—and we imagine how they move.

Leader: *Today when you listen to the story pay particular attention to how the characters might feel, sound, look, and move.*

Part 2: Character Image Selection and Visualization (20 Minutes)

Leader: *In a while you are going to write and perform story character dialogue. Dialogue is what characters say. You are **not** going to recite the character images as written on your handout; you are going to make up dialogue to go with the images. I would like each of you to select one of the 14 character images. The same character can have a different attitude in another scene or image. The way a character acts depends on what is going on in the story. Each image must be chosen.*

Give children the "Hawaiian StoryImage Vocabulary List (Transliterated)" handout, if they don't already have one; it can be found at the end of Program 1, above. Pronounce the Hawaiian words as transliterated and have the children repeat them several times. Give them the "Ohia and Lehua Story Character Images" handout. Have them choose an image with which to create dialogue and perform. Have the children read their chosen character image a couple of times to themselves. Then have them close their eyes and listen to what you say. Give them plenty of time between visualizations before going on to the next item.

Leader: *While keeping your eyes closed, I want you to imagine how your character looks in your character image . . . . Now I want you to imagine how he/she might smell . . . . Now I want you to imagine how he or she might feel inside . . . . Now I want you to imagine how he/she might sound* *and what he/she might say, when he or she speaks . . . . Now I want you to imagine how he or she might feel and move in this image.*

Part 3: Character Analysis, Dialogue Writing, and Collage (60 Minutes)

After the visualization, give the children a the "Character Analysis Worksheet" handout and review it with them, then have them fill it out. Ask them to write some dialogue in the first person to go with the selected character image. One or two sentences are fine. Have them memorize the dialogue they create, not the character image as written. Distribute the copies of the "Shapes" handout and have them cut out the shapes and create collages of their character. Have them draw details of the character within the shapes that best fit the shape of the character's head, arms, legs, and torso. They can recut once they have made the drawing inside the borders of the shapes, as long as the basic shapes are still obvious. Then have them arrange the shapes on the butcher paper and glue them to the paper. Have them write the dialogue that they created at the bottom of the page.

Part 4: Vocal and Movement Warm-up and Improvisation (40 Minutes)

Leader: *We are going to say each of the following vocal warm-up sounds three times each:*

> *Inhale, exhale slowly, making the Ommmmmm sound*
>
> *Inhale, exhale: Ma Me Mi Mo Mu*
>
> *Inhale, exhale: Ta Te Ti To Tu*
>
> *Inhale, exhale wolf yowl: Ah Ouuuuu*
>
> *Inhale, exhale: NeNeNeNe*
>
> *Inhale, exhale witch laugh: Ha! Ha! Ha! Ha! Ha!*

Now we will change the pitch and speed as we speak:

> Pitch: *I can speak very low; I can speak very high.*
>
> Speed: *Icanspeakquickly; I-can-speak-very-slowly.*

Now I want you to show the following moods in your voice and your face. We will do this all together. Start each time with "I am . . . ": I am happy; I am sad, I am angry, I am furious, I am calm, I am excited, I am self-confident, I am disappointed, I am in love, I am scared, I am cautious, I am tired. [Have the children practice the dialogue that they wrote for their character image again. Have them add an appropriate mood to their voices and facial expressions that fits with the character image in the story.]

*In a few minutes we are going to create movements from our feelings or moods. But first let's create our kinespheres, in which we will make these movements. Remember, a kinesphere is like a bubble that we create around our bodies. You will stay in your bubble. Your bubble is your personal space; you will be moving within your kinesphere, within your bubble, and you will **not** be moving across or around the room or touching others.*

[Tell the children to do the following (see "My Kinesphere" on page 124).]

- *Raise your arms to the side at shoulder level, parallel to the floor. Move apart so that you don't touch anyone else.*

- *Make one one-quarter turn to the right and again raise your arms to the side at shoulder level, parallel to the floor. Again adjust your space so that you are not touching anyone.*

- *Make another one-quarter turn to your right (you are opposite to where you started). Raise your arms as before.*

- *Make another one-quarter turn to your right and raise your arms as before.*

- *Make a final one-quarter turn to your right, facing front, where you started.*

- *Gently do the following; do not strain: Roll your body down by dropping your head forward, then your shoulders; ease your knees by bending them slightly, then roll down the rest of your back. Reverse slowly: roll up your back, keeping your head dropping heavily forward, and roll up your shoulders, then uncurl your neck as you raise your head to its normal position.*

[Give the children the following directions. Do not model, but rather let them create what they imagine. Remind them to stay in their bubble; their movements should not touch others.]

- *Draw a triangle in space with the following body parts as I call them out: your head, your shoulders, your arms, your elbows, and your hands.*

- *With your whole body create a triangle. Make it a very small triangle. Expand your triangle, making a very large triangle. Repeat, making your whole body triangular, smaller and larger, two more times. Repeat, making your whole body triangular, smaller and larger, two more times. The transition between the two sizes is very important, as this is how we see the formation take place.*

- *Draw a square in space with the following body parts as I call them out: your head, your shoulders, your arms, your elbows, and your hands.*

- *With your whole body create a square. Make it a very small square. Expand your square, making a very large square. Repeat, making your whole body square-shaped, smaller and larger, two more times.*

- *Draw a circle in space with the following body parts as I call them out: your head, your shoulders, your arms, your elbows, your hands, and your hips.*

- *With your whole body create a circle. Make it a very small circle. Expand your circle, making a very large circle.*

- *Draw your character image with your hand in the air and then step into the imaginary drawing, taking the shape of the character. Narrow and widen the shape. Again the transition between narrow and wide or large and small is very important, as this is how we see the object or setting form in front of our eyes.*

- *Instead of drawing it first, take the shape right away; become the shape, pause, and pose in that shape for a couple of moments. Once you have the correct size and form, do whatever the character might do, as the character might do it in that particular character selection.*

- *Take the shape and movement again, applying a mood to it; do the shape with what the character is feeling, such as happy, sad, angry, furious, calm excited, self-confident, disappointed, in love, scared, cautious, or tired.*

- *Memorize the dialogue that you've created, then glue the text to the bottom of your drawing and combine your movement with your spoken text. Add the mood to the spoken text. Work within a 2- to 3-foot square space.*

- *Now practice the mood that you selected for your dialogue with your movement and put the dialogue and movement together.*

Part 5: Presentations (35–45 Minutes)

Have children perform for the rest of the group their character images as rehearsed, taking the small shape and then animating it by moving into the large shape and then moving as the character moves in the image, using their selected mood, in the sequence in which the images appear in the story. They can refer to their pictures, and if they need to refer to the text, it will be visible at the bottom of their pictures.

Ohia and Lehua Story: Character Images

1. Ohia was a handsome young Hawaiian chief. He was a talented athlete. He was known for his athletic skills in boxing, wrestling, *holua* sled riding, and surf riding the ocean waves.

2. Pele the Goddess of the volcano thought that Ohia and she would make the perfect couple, and she was used to getting her own way.

3. Lehua was a beautiful girl; she knew Ohia loved her.

4. Ohia the handsome young chief climbed the *pali* to get stain for his surfboard from the Kukui bark. He stripped the bark off the tree.

5. Pele knows how to strip bark better than Ohia, so she instructs him. She knows the bark needs to be cut from the top down so the stain will make the surfboard slide, rather than jump into the air.

6. Pele is no stranger to the ways of the sea. She knows how to control the sea, making it smooth, or rolling gentle waves. She knows how to make curling waves, and thundering waves, and waves of destruction.

7. Pele admires Ohia's athletic skills and proposes to him.

8. Now that Ohia knows who she is, Ohia fears what Pele might do if he doesn't consent. He knows that she has the power to destroy the land and his people. He wants her to promise to hold back her powers.

9. Pele thinks Ohia is a wimp. She is surprised that this brave chief is filled with fear.

10. Ohia tries to reason with Pele. He tries to convince her that he is under the spell of love magic for Lehua. He thinks Lehua is having Pele, her goddess, test his love for Lehua.

11. Pele becomes enraged and has a fiery outburst of anger in which she transforms Ohia into a twisted tree with gray-green leaves.

12. Bird Catchers find the tree and see Ohia's tools and the cracked steaming earth nearby. They take the news to people about what Pele has done.

13. Lehua pleads with her goddess Pele to give Ohia back to his people and to take her life instead. No luck; Pele continues to fume.

14. The Gods try to revive Ohia. No luck. They transform Lehua into a blossom on the Ohia tree.

Character Analysis Worksheet

Make your comments apply to your particular image of your character; characters change how they look and act throughout the story.

1. **Looks:** My character looks like this: He or she is _____ feet tall, has _____ colored hair, is wearing _____. Other comments about how your character looks:

2. **Sounds:** My character's voice sounds like one or more of the following:

    Pitch: low, medium, high

    Speed: very slow, slow, average, fast, rapid.

3. **Feels:** Inside, my character is one or more of the following (circle): Happy, sad, in love, angry, scared, tired, cautious, furious, calm, excited, self-confident.

4. **Smells:** Choose one of the following (circle) or make one up: Like sweat, like smoky fire, like sweet perfume.

5. **Dialogue:** This is what my character says (write in the first person):

Program 3: Hawaiian StoryImage—Narration and Story Structure Interpretation

Summary

In this program the children select, visualize, and interpret one segment of the story, using the voice and motion of the narrator. They may add description to the segment. They perform the story segments in sequence for the other children in the group. It is recommended that students do either one or both of the prior two programs. Program 3 lasts about three and a half hours, including the introduction.

Program Preparation

Books

Use book and music lists from Program 1.

Space Needs

- Open space, about 2 square feet per child. Floor should be smooth: tiled or wood.
- Tables or desks and chairs, or cushions on floor with clipboards on which to write, glue, and draw

The environment should be free of interference noises such as those in a cafeteria.

Materials and Equipment

- CD and cassette player
- Pencils and crayons or colored pens
- Notebook paper to write what the children saw in their visualizations, for creating additional description of story incidents, and for other notes for narration improvisation.
- Glue sticks or tape
- Handouts:
    – "Narration and Story Structure" (at end of this section)
    – "Ohia and Lehua Story Outline" (at end of this section)
    – "Shapes" (at end of Program 1)

Before You Begin

- Gather all materials and equipment.
- Make copies of all handouts for each child. Make one enlarged copy (200 percent) of the "Ohia and Lehua Story Outline" and cut out each event for the children to paste or tape to the bottom portion of their collages.
- Review the program and handout contents.

Program

Introduction

> Welcome to the "Hawaiian StoryImage" workshop. Today our focus is on the narration part of the story. *Narration* is the act of giving an account describing incidents or a course of events. It does not contain dialogue but may contain emotion in describing characters, setting, or event. How you use your voice and how you move make it interesting. I am going to read or tell the Ohia and Lehua story today. The entire story is narrated. I am not going to be a character; I am going to be a narrator only. One can tell an entire story by narration, but dialogue makes it more interesting.

Leader: [Give the children a copy of the "Narration and Story Structure" handout.]

Story Structure. Most (not all) stories have a basic structure. The structure begins with an introduction. The introduction is followed by an initial incident. The initial incident is followed by the sequence of events. The sequence of events culminates at a high point. The story ends with a conclusion.

Introduction. The opening of a story, in which the characters and setting are introduced.

Initial incident. The first story event that sets off the other events; it triggers the rest of the action in the story.

Sequence of events. Events that make up the plot of the story: A leads to B, leads to C, etc.

High point. What A, B, C, etc., lead to; it is the most intense part of the story.

Conclusion. The resolution of the story and whatever issue was triggered in the initial incident.

As you hear the story today, see if you can identify the introduction, the initial incident, the sequence of events, the high point, and the conclusion.

Story Presentation (10 Minutes)

Leader: Mele *is sung poetry. I will play one about Pele, the Hawaiian Fire Goddess. Before and during the performance of an ancient hula (kahiko) in Hawaii, a* mele *is chanted. There are many* meles *and mo'olelo or stories for the Goddess Pele. When Pele gets angry, she becomes molten lava, erupting from the volcano and spewing down the side of the mountain toward the sea. Everything in her path is destroyed.*

The Ohia and Lehua Story

Read or tell "Ohia and Lehua."

Story Vocal and Movement Exercises

Part 1: Structure of the Ohia and Lehua Story (10 Minutes)

Leader: Let's look at Ohia and Lehua and see if we can identify its story structure. [Give the children an opportunity to answer and then follow up with the answers below.]

Introduction: What and who are introduced in the introduction of Ohia and Lehua?

Answer: The characters: Ohia and Pele are introduced. The setting: the Woods.

Initial incident: What triggers the rest of the action?

Answer: Pele's decision to have Ohia as her husband.

Sequence of events: What are the events in the plot?

Answer:

1. Ohia and a beautiful young woman meet in the woods.

2. The beautiful young woman reveals her true identity as the volatile fire goddess, Pele.

3. Pele tells Ohia that she has come to ask him to marry her.

4. Ohia is afraid to answer; he fears Lehua is having the goddess test his love for her, or maybe, if she is serious about marrying him and he refuses, Pele could be wrathful.

5. Ohia asks Pele to withhold her powers over the lightning and the volcano, when he answers her, to avoid bringing harm to himself and his people.

6. She promises, but teases him for being so weak.

7. She had other powers that she didn't tell him about. When he refuses, Pele becomes enraged and changes him into a tree.

8. Lehua pleads with Pele. Pele ignores her; she remains fuming in Halemaumau.

9. The Gods change Lehua into a blossom on the Ohia tree.

High point: What is the high point of this story?

Answer: When Pele turns Ohia into a tree.

Conclusion: What is the conclusion?

Answer: Lehua is turned into a blossom on the Ohia tree.

Part 2: Event Image Selection and Visualization

Give students the "Ohia and Lehua Story Outline" handout. Have them choose or assign them a section of narration from the introduction, initial incident, sequence of events, high point, or conclusion. All segments should be chosen. Have the children read their chosen segments a couple of times to themselves. Then have them close their eyes and listen to what you say. Give them plenty of time between visualizations before going on to the next item.

Leader: *While keeping your eyes closed, I want you to imagine what is happening in your segment of the story from the vantage point of the observer, the narrator. First, visualize what is going on, see it in your mind's eye . . . . Now I want you to imagine if there are any smells in the scene . . . . Now I want you to imagine the feeling or impact of the scene . . . . Can you hear any sounds, environmental sounds, or people speaking . . . ? Now I want you to imagine the action or movement going on in this segment of the story.*

Part 3: Descriptive Writing and Collage (60 Minutes)

Leader: *Now I want you to write and add any description of what you saw, smelled, felt, and heard in your visualization. Add description, not dialogue; you may also wish to add descriptive sounds said by the narrator.*

Distribute the copies of the "Shapes" handout (p. 127) and have the students cut out shapes of the event and draw details of the event within the shapes that best fit the action in the scene. They can recut once they have made the drawing inside the borders of the shapes, as long as the basic shapes are still obvious. Then have them arrange the shapes on the butcher paper and glue them to the paper. Have them leave space on the bottom of their pictures to glue any added description or sounds.

Part 4: Vocal and Movement Warm-up and Improvisation (40 Minutes)

Leader: *We will repeat each of the following three times. On the third one, project your voice across the room:*

> *Inhale, exhale slowly, making the Ommmmmm sound*
>
> *Inhale, exhale: Ma Me Mi Mo Mu*
>
> *Inhale, exhale: Ta Te Ti To Tu*
>
> *Inhale, exhale wolf yowl: Ah Ouuuuu*
>
> *Inhale, exhale: NeNeNeNe*
>
> *Inhale, exhale witch laugh: Ha! Ha! Ha! Ha! Ha!*

*Now we will create a kinesphere. After we do that, you will mirror narration images by copying my vocal intonations and a series of movements. Remember, a kinesphere is like a bubble that we create around our bodies. You will stay in your bubble. Your bubble is your personal space; you will be moving in place, within your bubble, and **not** be moving across or around the room or touching others.*

- *Raise your arms to the side at shoulder level, parallel to the floor. Move apart so that you don't touch anyone else.*

- *Make one one-quarter turn to the right and again raise your arms to the side at shoulder level, parallel to the floor. Again adjust your space so that you are not touching anyone.*

- *Make another one-quarter turn to your right (you are opposite to where you started). Raise your arms as before.*

- *Make another one-quarter turn to your right and raise your arms as before.*

- *Make a final one-quarter turn to your right, facing front, where you started.*

- *Gently do the following; do not strain: Roll your body down by dropping your head forward, then your shoulders; ease your knees by bending them slightly, then roll down the rest of your back. Reverse slowly: roll up your back, keeping your head dropping heavily forward, and roll up your shoulders, then uncurl your neck as you raise your head to its normal position.*

Now we are going to create movement based on narration in the story. [Give children the following directions. Do not model them, but rather let them create what they imagine. Remind them to stay in their bubble; their movement should not touch others.]:

- *Draw a triangle in space with the following body parts as I call them out: your head, your shoulders, your arms, your elbows, and your hands.*

- *With your whole body create a triangle. Make it a very small triangle. Expand your triangle, making a very large triangle. Repeat, making your whole body triangular, smaller and larger, two more times. Repeat, making your whole body triangular, smaller and larger, two more times. The transition between the two sizes is very important, as this is how we see the formation take place.*

- *Draw a square in space with the following body parts as I call them out: your head, your shoulders, your arms, your elbows, and your hands.*

- *With your whole body create a square. Make it a very small square. Expand your square, making a very large square. Repeat, making your whole body square-shaped, smaller and larger, two more times.*

- *Draw a circle in space with the following body parts as I call them out: your head, your shoulders, your arms, your elbows, your hands, and your hips.*

- *With your whole body create a circle. Make it a very small circle. Expand your circle, making a very large circle.*

- *Draw an action going on in your event image with your hand in the air and then step into the imaginary drawing, taking the shapes of the action in your setting. Narrow and widen the shape. Again, the transition between narrow and wide or large and small is very important, as this is how we see the event form in front of our eyes.*

- *Instead of drawing it first, take the shape right away; become the shape, pause, and pose in that shape for a couple of moments. Once you have the correct size and form, do whatever is happening in the event. Take the shape and movement again, applying the mood of the event to it, such as happy, sad, angry, furious, calm, exciting, disappointed, fearful, or loving.*

• *Memorize the text of your image, glue it to the bottom of your drawing, and combine your movement with your spoken text. Add a mood to the spoken text. Work within a 2- to 3-foot square space.*

Part 4: Presentations (45 Minutes)

Have the children perform for the rest of the group their event images as rehearsed, taking the small shape and then animating it by moving into the large shape and then moving as the object moves, using their selected mood, in the sequence in which the image appears in the story. If they need to refer to the text, it will be visible at the bottom of their pictures.

Narration and Story Structure

Narration

Narration is the act of describing incident**s** or a course of events. It does not contain dialogue but can contain intense emotion. How you use your voice and move make it interesting. One can tell an entire story by narration, but dialogue makes it livelier. Narration is also exciting when you add descriptive sounds.

Story Structure

A *story structure* is the framework of a story.

An *introduction* is the opening of a story, in which the characters and setting are introduced.

The *initial incident* is the first story event that sets off the other events; it triggers the rest of the action in the story.

The *sequence of events* makes up the plot of the story: A leads to B, leads to C, etc.

The *high point* is what A, B, C, etc., lead to; it is the most intense part of the story.

The *conclusion* is the resolution of the story and whatever issue was triggered in the initial incident.

Ohia and Lehua Story Outline

1. **Introduction:** Ohia and a beautiful young woman meet in the woods.

2. The beautiful young woman reveals her true identity as the volatile fire goddess, Pele.

3. **Initial incident:** Pele tells him that she has come to ask him to marry her.

Other incidents:

4. Ohia is afraid to answer; he fears Lehua is having the goddess test his love for her or maybe, if she is serious about marrying him and he refuses, she could be wrathful.

5. Ohia asks Pele to withhold her powers over the lightning and the volcano, when he answers her, to avoid bringing harm to himself and his people.

6. She promises, but teases him for being so weak.

7. **High point:** Pele had other powers that she didn't tell him about. When he refuses, Pele becomes enraged and changes him into a tree.

8. Lehua pleads with Pele. Pele ignores her; she remains fuming in Halemaumau.

9. **Conclusion:** The Gods change Lehua into a blossom on the Ohia tree.

 From *Stories on the Move: Integrating Literature and Movement with Children, Infants to Age 14* by Arlene Cohen. Illustrated by Andrea Fitcha McAllister. Westport, CT: Libraries Unlimited. Copyright © 2007.

Program 4: Poetry StoryImage—Selection, Analysis, and Memorization

Summary

In "Moving Poetry" Program 4 the children select, visualize, analyze, and memorize a poem. They will perform an animated poem in Program 5. This program lasts about two hours. The "Moving Poetry" two-part workshop can be done separately or build upon the three "Hawaiian StoryImage" programs.

Program Preparation

Books

- Prelutsky, Jack. "As Soon as Fred Gets out of Bed." In *Something BIG Has Been Here*. Illustrated by James Stevenson. New York: Greenwillow Books, 1990.

Additional Books for Children's Poetry Selection (Humorous Poems)

- Prelutsky, Jack, comp. *For Laughing Out Loud: Poems to Tickle your Funnybone*. Illustrated by Marjorie Priceman. New York: Knopf, distributed by Random House, 1991.

- Prelutsky, Jack, comp. *Imagine That!: Poems of Never-Was*. Illustrated by Kevin Hawkes. New York: Knopf, distributed by Random House, 1998.

- Silverstein, Shel. *A Light in the Attic*. New York: HarperCollins, [2001], 1981.

- Silverstein, Shel. *Where the Sidewalk Ends: The Poems & Drawings of Shel Silverstein*. New York: HarperCollins, [2000].

Music

Vocal expressiveness replaces recorded music in this program.

Space Needs

There is no movement in this program. The environment should be free of interference noises such as those in a cafeteria.

Materials and Equipment

- Chairs and tables or desks on which to write, glue, and draw
- Pencils and crayons or colored pens
- Glue sticks or scotch tape

- Paper for writing what the children see in their visualizations
- Handouts:
    - "Narration and Story Structure" (at end of Program 3)
    - "Step-by-Step Plan for Memorizing a Poem" (at end of this chapter)
    - "Poetry Analysis Worksheet" (at end of this section)
    - "Shapes" (at end of Program 1)

Before You Begin

- Review the program and handout contents.
- Read or rehearse the sample poem and the poem analysis below, or make up your own analysis by filling out the "Poetry Analysis Worksheet."
- Copy poems from poetry books and place them in a notebook for children to select and copy. If possible, give children an opportunity to select their poem a few days ahead of the workshop.
- Gather all materials.
- Make copies of handouts, one for each child.
- Make several copies of the "Shapes" handout for each child.

Program

Introduction

> Welcome to Part 1 of the "Moving Poetry" workshop." Today you will select, visualize, analyze, and memorize a poem. In Part 2 of the "Moving Poetry" workshop you will bring your poem's images to life by creating animated shapes. I will tell you more about that next time.

Leader: *A poem contains images, or mental pictures of how the characters, setting, or events look, sound, feel, taste, and move.* [Give the children the "Narration and Story Structure" handout.]

Poems may or may not tell a story. They are composed of images like a story and usually have strong emotion, purpose, and rhythm. Poems are written in stanzas. A stanza is a division of a poem, composed of two or more lines, usually characterized by a common pattern of meter, rhyme, and number of lines. Setting, character, or event may be the main or only image.

Poems may or may not have all the images that a story has: characters, settings, and events. Frequently they do not have a distinct introduction, conclusion, or plot, as most stories do. Here is how a story is structured; you may refer to your handout to see if the poem has any of the following story elements:

- **_Introduction:_** _the opening of the story, in which the characters and setting are introduced._

- **_Initial incident:_** _an event that triggers the rest of the action in the story._

- **_Plot_**_: a sequence of events; A leads to B, B leads to C, etc._

- **_High point:_** _the most intense part of the story._

- **_Conclusion:_** _a resolution._

Narration _is the act of giving an account describing incidents or a course of events. It does not contain dialogue but can contain intense emotion. How you use your voice and how you move make it interesting. Poems may have only narration, or only dialogue, or a combination of both. As I read or perform the following poem, see if you can identify a setting, characters, events, narration, dialogue, an introduction, an initial incident, a high point, and a conclusion._

Poem Presentation (2 Minutes)

Read or perform the poem "As Soon as Fred Gets out of Bed," by Jack Prelutsky.

Poetry Exercises

Part 1: Poem Analysis (10 Minutes)

Give the children an opportunity to answer, and confirm with the following answers below.

Leader: _Are there settings and objects in this poem?_

Answer: Fred's bedroom, morning and night. A bed, underwear, a light switch, his head, his toes.

Leader: _Is there a character(s) in this poem? What is the personality of the character(s)?_

Answer: Fred, a silly/funny little boy who likes to play games. Fred's mother, who has a good sense of humor.

Leader: _Is there narration in this poem? Is there dialogue?_

Answer: Yes, all the things Fred does are narrated; he doesn't speak. His mother's actions are narrated, and also she speaks twice, when she tells Fred not to put his underwear on his head and when she says good night.

Leader: _Is there a plot or sequence of events in this poem?_

Answer: Six condensed incidents: Fred gets up, he puts underwear on his head, his mother says not to do that, he wears it on his head all day anyway, his mother says goodnight, and Fred puts the underwear on his toes.

Leader: _Is there a high point?_

Answer: The initial incident seems to be the high point, when Fred first puts the underwear on his head.

Leader: *Is there a conclusion?*

Answer: Fred's underwear goes on his toes.

Part 2: Poem Selection and Visualization (15 Minutes)

Give the children a poem, if they haven't already selected one ahead of time. Ask them to read their poem a couple of times to themselves. Have them close their eyes; take a couple of deep breaths and slowly exhale before listening quietly to what you say. Give them plenty of time between each visualization before going on to the next one.

Leader: *While keeping your eyes closed, I want you to imagine how your characters look, what they might be wearing . . . how the settings and the objects in the settings look . . . how the events look . . . . Now I want you to imagine how your characters might feel inside . . . how the settings and the objects in your settings might feel when you touch them. Now I want you to imagine how your characters talk . . . can you hear any sounds in the settings? Last, imagine how your characters and objects move in your poem.*

Part 3: Selected Poem Analysis and Collage (60 Minutes)

Review the "Poetry Analysis Worksheet" with the children and have them answer the questions.

Distribute the copies of the "Shapes" handout (p. 127) and have the children cut out shapes of the events, which include the characters and settings in the events. There will be one picture for each event. Have them draw details of the event within the shapes that best fit the action in the scene. They can cut once they have made the drawing inside the borders of the shapes, as long as the basic shapes are still obvious. Then have them arrange the shapes on the butcher paper and glue them to the paper.

Part 4: Memorization (30 Minutes)

Give the children the "Step-by-Step Plan for Memorizing a Poem" handout (at end of this chapter). Show them how to memorize a couple of poetry phrases. Then have them memorize their poem. Ask them to keep practicing their poem several times before the second "Poetry StoryImage" workshop and to think of a simple costume that they can make and wear for the performance. Ask them to bring the costume or idea for Program 5.

Make copies of or keep the completed handouts and notated poems, in case they forget to bring them next time.

Poetry Analysis Worksheet

1. **Describe the characters in your poem:** How do they look, talk, and move? What might the main character in your story be wearing, if you were to design a costume for that character?

2. **Describe the settings/objects in your poem:** How do they look, sound, and possibly move?

3. **If there is an introduction in your poem?** Describe who, where, and what is introduced.

4. **List the events in your poem.**

5. **Label the events in number 4 above** as initial incident, high point, and conclusion, if they are present in your poem.

Program 5: Poetry StoryImage—Improvisation and Performance

Summary

As a follow-up to Program 4, the children have a vocal and movement warm-up and a rehearsal in which they animate the shapes of the images in their poems, to perform for an audience: other children, families, the school, the library, or the community. This program lasts about two hours. I suggest several rehearsals for you to coach them for the performance and one rehearsal to make costumes.

Program Preparation

Books

- Prelutsky, Jack. "As Soon as Fred Gets out of Bed." In *Something BIG Has Been Here*. Illustrated by James Stevenson. New York: Greenwillow Books, 1990.

Space Needs

- Open space, about 2 or 3 square feet per child. Floor should be smooth: tiled or wood.

The environment should be free of interference noises such as those in a cafeteria.

Materials and Equipment

- Tables or desks and chairs, or cushions on floor with clipboards on which to write, glue, and draw
- Hand drum or sealed empty oatmeal box and large wooden spoon
- Microphones, lavaliere if available, one for every three children
- Pencils or pens
- Completed handouts from Part 1 of the poetry workshop

Before You Begin

- Gather all materials and equipment.
- Review and practice the program.

Program

Poetry Vocal and Movement Exercises

Part 1: Vocal Exercises (5 Minutes)

Leader: *Say each of the following three times. On the third time, project your voice across the room:*

Inhale, exhale slowly, making the Ommmmmm sound

Inhale, exhale: Ma Me Mi Mo Mu

Inhale, exhale: Ta Te Ti To Tu

Inhale, exhale wolf yowl: Ah Ouuuuu

Inhale, exhale: NeNeNeNe

Inhale, exhale witch laugh: Ha! Ha! Ha! Ha! Ha!

Part 2: Movement Exercises (30 Minutes)

Have the children form a circle initially to walk around the room as you keep time with the drum.

Leader:

1. *Walk clockwise around the circumference of the room a few times.* [Play the drum, accenting every count: 1-2-3-4-5-6-7-8; repeat several times at a moderate tempo.]

2. *Spinal alignment: Stop and roll your upper body down from the top of your head, one vertebra at a time. Use all eight counts to roll down.* [Count out loud: 1-2-3-4-5-6-7-8.] *Let your head hang heavily and slightly bend your knees to avoid straining your back. Make a hissing sound while you hang forward for eight counts, dangling your arms and imagining water rolling off your back onto the floor. Slowly uncurl your body, one vertebra at a time from the base of your spine to eight counts.* [Count out loud: 1-2-3-4-5-6-7-8.] *As before, your head should hang heavily until after you've uncurled your shoulders and neck.*

3. *Walk counterclockwise around the room a few times.* [Play the drum, accenting every count: 1-2-3-4-5-6-7-8; repeat several times at a moderate tempo.]

4. *Walk faster and faster and faster.* [Gradually increase the tempo, still accenting every count.]

5. *Now, begin to slow down, slower, slower, slower.* [Gradually decrease the tempo, accenting every count.] *Stop. Shake out your arms and legs.*

[Give the children the following directions; do not model them, but rather let them create what they imagine. Remind them to stay in their own space; their movement should not touch others.]:

- *Draw a triangle in space with the following body parts as I call them out: your head, your shoulders, your arms, your elbows, and your hands.*

- *With your whole body create a triangle. Make it a very small triangle. Expand your triangle, making a very large triangle. Repeat, making your whole body triangular, smaller and larger, two more times. Repeat, making your whole body triangular, smaller and larger, two more times. The transition between the two sizes is very important, as this is how we see the formation take place.*

- *Draw a square in space with the following body parts as I call them out: your head, your shoulders, your arms, your elbows, and your hands.*

- *With your whole body create a square. Make it a very small square. Expand your square, making a very large square. Repeat, making your whole body square-shaped, smaller and larger, two more times.*

- *Draw a circle in space with the following body parts as I call them out: your head, your shoulders, your arms, your elbows, your hands, and your hips.*

- *With your whole body create a circle. Make it a very small circle. Expand your circle, making a very large circle.*

- *Draw an event image from your poem with your hand in the air and then step into the imaginary drawing, taking the shape of the event. Narrow and widen the shape. Again, the transition between narrow and wide or large and small is very important, as this is how we see the event form in front of our eyes.*

- *Instead of drawing it first, take the event shape right away; become the shape, pause, and pose in that shape for a couple of moments. Once you have the correct size and form, do whatever happens in that event.*

- *Take the shape and movement again, applying a mood to it; do the shape with feeling or a mood, such as happy, sad, peaceful, angry, afraid, or funny.*

Part 3: Improvisation (30 Minutes)

Have the children practice their poems with poses and animation of the poem events.

Leader: *Apply the moods to your spoken text when you practice.*

Part 4: Rehearsals (45 Minutes)

Have each child perform his or her poem for this group. Rotate microphones, preferably lavaliere if available. Schedule more rehearsals if you are planning a performance, as many as you feel the children need. One rehearsal should include making a costume.

Program 6: Mirrors of Trees

Summary

We now proceed to a new and separate "StoryImage" program, unrelated to the previous programs in this chapter. The children hear a story, hear a poem, do dance improvisations, do creative writing, and draw to develop an awareness of our interdependence with trees and plants for health and well-being. It is best done outdoors, but indoors will also work. After hearing a story about trees the children have a creative writing exercise about what they would do if there weren't any more trees or plants. Then they do a guided movement improvisation on the growth cycle of a tree. They select a tree to sketch. They create choreography from their sketches, which is used for solo and group dances. The program ends with a group breathe circle. The program lasts about two and a half to three hours. To do it in less time, eliminate one or more parts.

Program Preparation

Book

- Silverstein, Shel. *The Giving Tree*. New York: HarperCollins, [2004], c1992.

Space Needs

- Outdoor flat space in a park or area where there are several deciduous trees with interesting branch formations

Materials and Equipment

- If done indoors: clear colored large photos or projected slides of the same trees from three different angles and a projector and screen
- Drawing pads or paper and charcoal or pencils for each child
- Handout: "Imagine a World Without Plants" (at end of this section)
- Clipboards and pencils for children to use for filling out the handout and for making drawings

Before You Begin

- Review the program.
- Make a copy of the handout for each child.
- Gather all materials.
- Set up the projector and screen if doing the program indoors.

Program

Introduction

> Welcome to "Mirrors of Trees." Today we are going to have fun appreciating and re-creating trees through creative writing, drawing, and movement.

Sitting under the shade of a tree (if possible), read or tell *The Giving Tree*.

Story Writing, Drawing, and Movement Exercises

Part 1: Plant Stories (30 Minutes)

Ask children what they thought about the story and what they think about trees. Have them fill out the story form "Imagine a World Without Plants." Ask for volunteers to read their stories.

Part 2: Growth Cycle of a Tree (30 Minutes)

Encourage children to use their legs, feet, torso, arms, and hands to create the following images from standing positions. Tell them to think of their feet as their roots, their legs and torso as their trunk, and their arms and head as their branches. They should *not* go down on all fours to the ground and crawl around. All movement should be slow and should be posed when the motion is complete.

Leader:

1. *The seed falls onto the ground.*

2. *The seed spreads roots.*

3. *The seedling sprouts out of the ground.*

4. *The trunk grows wider.*

5. *Branches grow and extend from the trunk.*

6. *Leaves form on the branches.*

7. *The trunk grows taller.*

8. *The branches sway in the wind.*

9. *A cold rainstorm comes and rumbles the ground, slashing at the tree; the tree roots hold strongly to the ground.*

10. *The wind subsides and the sun comes out; the leaves open to the warmth of the sun.*

11. *Over the years, the tree grows into a tall and lovely, wide shade tree.*

12. *The tree drops a seed on the ground.*

Part 3: The Dancer in the Tree (20 Minutes)

Leader: [Read the poem to the children:]

The Dancer in the Tree (original poem)

Trees are very special

just like you and me.

They have lots to give

just like you and me.

They give shade and clear the air,

Provide food and homes for birds and other animals,

and pretty flowers to smell and wear.

Trees are special because each one is different

just like you and me.

Some trees are very straight and tall;

some are crooked and small

and within each tree is a dancer,

just like you and me.

Can you see the dancer in the tree?

Have children pick one tree to sketch. The drawing should be only a simple outline of the trunk and branches, and roots, if exposed, that is, the shapes of the tree. Have them draw the tree from three angles. Before they begin, have them sit quietly in front of the tree and study it carefully. Have them look at the tree slowly from bottom to top and imagine how it formed into the shape that it has. Have them study the roots or imagine them if they are not visible, how the trunk is formed, which way it leans, and the angles and shapes of the branches.

Part 4: Tree Perspectives (1 Hour)

Single Person Tree Dance

Before performing for the group, have the children practice the following. Have them start from a seed in a curled up standing position and then unfurl into the shapes of the three drawn perspectives, each time curling back into the seed. On the fourth unfurl, they release into whatever shape comes through them or to them, that is, whatever comes naturally.

Tree Perspectives.

Grove Dance

Create movement space by having the children:

1. Raise their arms to the side at shoulder level, parallel to the floor. They should move apart so that they don't touch anyone else.

2. Make one one-quarter turn to the right and again raise their arms to the side at shoulder level, parallel to the floor. Again adjust their space so that they are not touching anyone.

3. Make another one-quarter turn to their right (they are opposite to where they started). Raise their arms as before.

4. Make another one-quarter turn to their right and raise their arms as before.

5. Make a final one-quarter turn to their right, facing front where they started.

6. Have them take an additional four steps apart; they will be spreading their branches.

Now they will re-create what they did in the solo dances. Remind them to unfurl slowly. This time they will do their dances simultaneously, as a grove of trees. When each person finishes his or her angle and final movement, have them all remain in that shape, until all are done. They do not all need to be doing the same angle at the same time.

Composite Tree

In groups of three to five, have the children get close enough so that one of their legs is touching the leg of the others, forming one tree trunk.

Composite Tree.

Now they will re-create the previous angles and final movement as one tree, by always keeping the multi-legged trunk together. Of course they will be adjusting their movements as they do in sharing their lives with others.

Part 5: Group Breathe (5–10 Minutes)

Have the children form a circle, their palms touching the center of the back of the person next to them. Have everyone inhale and bend their knees and then exhale and go up on the balls of their feet (not their toes), just raising their heels off the ground. After doing four sets of up and down, widen the circle slowly until they are all touching fingertips with the person next to them. Have them let go of the person next to them, dropping their arms to their sides and standing in place for a couple moments of silence with their eyes closed. Ask them to open their eyes and then place their palms together and bow to the center of the circle.

Imagine a World Without Plants

Fill in the blanks at the end of each sentence to complete your story:

1. One day I woke up and there were no trees, no plants of any kind. When I looked out of the window all I saw was _____

_____

_____

2. The reason there were no trees or plants was _____

_____

_____

3. Because there were no trees or plants, I had trouble breathing. I had to put on an oxygen suit so I could breathe. This is what my oxygen suit looked like: _____

_____

_____

4. Since most food comes from plants, I had a very unusual dinner. I ate

_____

_____

5. Later I met my friend and went to climb trees in the park, but there were no trees to climb. So instead we _____

_____

_____

6. We found some plant seeds, so we _____

_____

_____

From *Stories on the Move: Integrating Literature and Movement with Children, Infants to Age 14* by Arlene Cohen. Illustrated by Andrea Fitcha McAllister. Westport, CT: Libraries Unlimited. Copyright © 2007.

Step-by-Step Plan for Memorizing a Poem

1. Read the whole thing

2. Read and memorize a few words or a line at a time

3. Read the few words or line aloud to yourself

4. Read the few words or line to yourself

5. Close your eyes and say the few words or line aloud

6. Read it again to see if you missed anything; if you did repeat the process

7. Move onto the next few words or line and repeat the process

8. Close your eyes and see what you remember from what you have practiced so far

9. Learn a little more in the same way and then again add the new part onto what you remember by closing your eyes and saying the whole thing aloud

10. Once you have memorized your poem, you will be free to play with how you express it through your voice and movement.

Chapter 6

Moving Stories and Fables: Ages Twelve to Fourteen

Introduction

In this chapter children hear, practice, and perform moving stories and fables. In the three-part "workshop," "Moving Stories," children learn about story elements and story structure and are given instruction on aligning voice and movement to bring to life a story image of characters, settings, and events. They perform a short moving image passage in each of the three parts of the program. If the leader of the program does not have a background in storytelling and wishes to perform the literature, see the "Trigger Method of Learning a Story (Group Leader)" handout at the end of this chapter. If the leader does or doesn't have a background in dance, the "Moving Stories" program explains how to create movement for story imagery. The "Moving Stories" program lays the groundwork for the "Moving Fables performance program." In "Moving Fables" children tell a whole fable that they have reconstructed, adding or deleting story elements. They rehearse key words and phrases and a series of events to add spontaneity to their performance, as storytellers do. The "Moving Fables" can be assembled for a performance for a larger audience.

The goal is to perform a vivid story image by infusing the spoken word and the movement with the energy quality of a mood. For example, if the child interprets the mood of the image as happy, he or she may perform that by using both voice and movement to convey a floating or gliding energy. An exuberant mood can also burst through the voice and movement. Nonverbal communication is as important as verbal communication in these programs. The movement vocabulary that children develop allows them to speak through their body movements. How and what movements are emphasized and the degree of intensity of the movements convey the same message as the words used in conjunction with them.

Details about 12- to 14-year-olds' cognitive and physical skills are outlined in Table 6.1.

163

Table 6.1. Readiness to Learn (12- to 14-Year-Olds)

COGNITIVE	PHYSICAL
➢ Exhibits increased abstract thought ➢ Can creatively interpret story imagery using energy qualities ➢ Experiences subtleties of emotions: mood and tone ➢ Uses figures of speech such as metaphors and similes ➢ Can learn a story by rehearsing key words and phrases, instead of memorizing. ➢ Visualizes story elements ➢ Understands story structure	➢ Can create a sequence of refined movements and repeat them ➢ Is aware of and creatively uses personal and general space for movement ➢ Can create moving images of story elements ➢ Can modulate voice

Handouts that can be used in several programs are included at the end of this chapter; those that pertain only to one program can be found immediately following the program.

Program 1: Moving Stories—Characters

Summary

In this first part of a three-part workshop, selected passages from a translation of "The Little Mermaid" for older children serve as the catalyst for learning how to align voice and movement to bring images of story characters to life. Each of the programs—"Characters," "Settings," and "Events"—takes about two to two and a half hours. The programs build on each other and should be done in sequence. If you wish to perform, rather than read the story, see the "Trigger Method of Learning a Story (Group Leader)" handout at the end of this chapter.

Program Preparation

Books

- Andersen, Hans Christian. "The Little Mermaid." In *Fairy Tales*. Translated by Tiina Nunnally. Edited and introduced by Jackie Wullschlager. New York: Viking, 2005. The Little Mermaid would gladly give up her lifespan of 300 years, if she could be a human girl and win the love of the Prince and an immortal soul.

Alternative Resources

- Andersen, Hans Christian. *The Little Mermaid.* Translated from the Danish by Anthea Bell. Illustrated by Lisbeth Zwerger. New York: Minedition/Penguin, 2004.

- Andersen, Hans Christian. *Little Mermaid and Ugly Duckling: Favorite Fairytales.* Illustrated by Gennady Spirin. San Francisco: Chronicle Books, 2001.

Music

- "Malibu Surf" and other ocean sounds, from *Hush Little Baby: Soothing Sounds for Sleep.* Pacific Palisades, CA: Kids Music Factory, 2003.

Space Needs

- Two to three square feet of uncarpeted open space for each child.

- Tables or desks and chairs on the side for each child or seating on the floor, with cushions and a hard surface on which to write.

The environment should be free of interference noises such as those in a cafeteria.

Materials and Equipment

- CD and cassette player

- Percussion instrument: flat hand drum with drumstick or empty oatmeal box and large wooden spoon

- Handouts:
    - "Character Statement Selections" (at end of this section)
    - "Character Image Worksheet" (at end of this section)
    - "Character Image Worksheet Sample" (at end of this section)

- Microphones, preferably lavalieres, to rotate as children perform

- Pencils or pens for each child

- Small sticky notes

- One hard writing surface such as clipboard or book, for each child (if they are writing while sitting on floor)

Before You Begin

- Copy the "Practice Character Statement" handout at the end of this section (one copy to hold up during the vocal exercise): "Grandmother, if people do not drown, do they live until the end of time?"

- Place sticky notes on selected passages for performing:

    – The introduction to the story up to "her body ended in a fishtail."

    – Grandmother informing the sea princesses about turning 15 and seeing life above the sea.

    – The Little Mermaid turns 15 and rises above the sea.

    – The Little Mermaid sees and rescues the Prince and places him on shore, where he is found by another young girl.

    – The Little Mermaid asks Grandmother about immortality.

    – The Little Mermaid seeks the help of the Sea Witch, including her passage to where the Sea Witch lives.

    – The Little Mermaid drinks the potion to grow legs and is met by the Prince on land.

    – The Prince weds another and The Little Mermaid despairs.

    – The Sisters give her a knife to regain her fishtail by stabbing the Prince.

    – The Little Mermaid decides not to stab the Prince and throws the knife and herself into the ocean.

    – The Little Mermaid is transformed into a daughter of the air.

- To perform the story, see the "Trigger Method of Learning a Story (Group Leader)" handout at the end of this chapter.

- To create movement to go with the text, follow the process for doing this, as outlined in the program.

- Practice the workshop activities.

- Make copies of each handout for each child.

- Gather and set up the equipment and materials.

Program

Introduction

> Welcome to the "Moving Stories" workshop, Part 1. Today you will learn how to perform images of characters. Before we begin, I'd like to talk to you a bit about figurative language: similes. A simile is a figure of speech in which a word or phrase connotes that something is *like* something else, thus making an implicit comparison. "The Little Mermaid" story, as originally told by Hans Christian Andersen, is a story for older children. In the story today, the sea is *like* a prison to The Little Mermaid. Because she cannot have what she wants there, she feels locked up, confined. Another ex-

ample is the statement that The Little Mermaid's skin is "soft *like* a rose petal." Even though you can't touch the skin of The Little Mermaid, most likely you've touched a rose petal and know how soft that is. The author uses similes in the text of the story to "color" how characters, settings, and events appear, so that the audience or reader can readily relate to them by association with something familiar. Similarly, in performing a moving story image, we color our voices and movements with qualities of energy or moods, so that the audience can feel and relate to the image. For example, we can color our voices and movements with a sense of the pressing confinement of a prison or the gliding softness of the mermaid's skin. This coloring process is how one aligns voice and motions. In this workshop you will learn how to align voice with movement to create vivid literary imagery. We align voice and movement by paying attention to the moods or feelings present in characters, settings, and events. We express these moods verbally and nonverbally to send the same message with our voices and movements. We speak with our bodies, just as we speak with our voices. We do this naturally all the time. The only difference in performing moving stories from what we do everyday is that we project our voices and exaggerate our movements for our audience.

Story Presentation (10 Minutes)

Play "Malibu Surf" in the background to set the mood. Stop the ocean sounds after the story introduction, for example, after the following story text: "her body ended in a fishtail."

Read or perform the selected passages from "The Little Mermaid."

Story Vocal and Movement Exercises

Part 1: Vocal Exercises (10 Minutes)

Leader: *Before each of the following, inhale deeply, and as you exhale make the sounds to warm up your voice, which start down in your abdomen, move up through your chest, through your vocal cords, and out through your mouth and nose. Make each sound three times, inhaling between each repetition:*

Inhale, exhale slowly, making the Ommmmmm sound

Inhale, exhale: Ma Me Mi Mo Mu

Inhale, exhale: Ta Te Ti To Tu

Inhale, exhale wolf yowl: Ah Ouuuuu

Inhale, exhale: NeNeNeNe

Inhale, exhale witch laugh: Ha! Ha! Ha! Ha! Ha!

Vocal Variations

Leader: [Hold up the "Practice Character Statement."] *Here is something The Little Mermaid might have said: "Grandmother, if people do not drown, do they live until the end of time?" Now I want you to say this line, using different mood or energy qualities, one by one, as I call them out. Please feel free to use whatever facial expressions or gestures naturally come with your voice. Say it as follows:*

- *Peaceful/floating: Sustained or slow and light, sense of rising up*

- *Happy/gliding: Sustained or slow and light, level or even*

- *Impatient/pressing: Sustained or slow and strong, forward direction*

- *Sad/dragging: Sustained or slow and strong with down direction*

- *Nervous or afraid/dabbing: Sudden or quick and light, at something, tic-like*

- *Agitated/flicking: Sudden or quick and light, anywhere in space*

- *Angry/slashing: Sudden or quick and strong, anywhere in space*

Which variation(s) do you think work(s) best in this situation, considering the author's intention? [Give the students time to respond and say why they chose that mood or energy quality for that sentence.]

Part 2: Statement Selection (30 Minutes)

- Give children the "Character Statement Selections" handout. Assign or have them choose one of the statements for their improvisation. If there are enough children, all the statements should be selected.

- Have them learn the statement. They can change words as long as they mean the same thing. They don't have to memorize it word for word. It is more natural if they do put it in their own words; encourage them to do this.

- Give children the "Character Image Worksheet" and the "Character Image Worksheet Sample." Go over the sample and their worksheet and have them answer the first three questions.

- Have them practice their own selection using the vocal variations, and then answer question 4 on the "Character Image Worksheet." They may refer to the "Character Image Worksheet Sample."

Part 3: Movement Exercises (15 Minutes)

Leader: [Ask children to do the following:]

1. *Walk clockwise around the circumference of the room a few times.* [Play the drum, accenting every count: 1-2-3-4-5-6-7-8; repeat several times, at a moderate tempo.]

2. *Spinal alignment: Stop.* [Demonstrate the following for them before they do it; be sure to bend your knees slightly as you roll down.] *Roll your upper body down*

from the top of your head, one vertebra at a time; bend your knees slightly as you roll down. Use all 8 counts to roll down. [Count out loud: 1-2-3-4-5-6-7-8.] *Let your head hang forward heavily. Make hissing sounds while you hang you head forward for eight counts, dangling your arms and imagining water rolling off your back onto the floor. Slowly uncurl your body, one vertebra at a time from the base of your spine, up at eight counts.* [Count out loud: 1-2-3-4-5-6-7-8] *As before, your head should hang forward heavily until after you've uncurled your shoulders and neck.*

3. *Walk counterclockwise around the room a few times.* [Play the drum, accenting every count: 1-2-3-4-5-6-7-8; repeat several times, at a moderate tempo.]

4. *Walk faster and faster and faster.* [Gradually increase the tempo, still accenting every count.]

5. *Now, begin to slow down, slower, slower, slower.* [Gradually decrease the tempo, accenting every count.] *Stop. Shake out your arms and legs.*

[Have everyone face you. They should remain spread around the room.] *We are going to square off now, so everyone will have adequate room to move in their personal space:*

1. *Raise your arms to the side, palms down, at shoulder level, parallel to the floor. Move apart so that you don't touch anyone else.*

2. *Make a one-quarter turn to the right and again raise your arms to the side at shoulder level, parallel to the floor. Again adjust your space so that you are not touching anyone.*

3. *Make another one-quarter turn to your right (you are opposite to where you started). Raise your arms as before.*

4. *Make another one-quarter turn to your right and raise your arms as before.*

5. *Make a final one-quarter turn to your right, facing front where you started.*

Now I'm going to ask you to move parts of your body using a mood or energy quality. The first three mood or energy qualities are slow or sustained.

1. *Peaceful/floating: Sustained or slow and light, sense of rising up*

   Let your arms slowly float up from your sides as if they were being inflated with air. Now "float" your head off your shoulders.

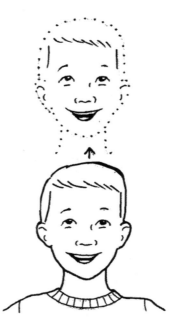

Floating Head.

Be The Little Mermaid rising slowly up, up, like a bubble, to the surface of the water.

2.   *Happy/gliding: Sustained or slow and light, level or even*

Now glide your hands as if you were running them over a smooth surface. The Little Mermaid's skin is as soft as a rose petal.

Gliding a Hand over a Smooth Surface.

Bend your knees and glide your hips like a hula dancer.

3. *Impatient/pressing: Sustained or slow and strong, forward direction*

Press your head and chest forward, as if seeking Grandmother to answer the first part of this important question: "Grandmother, oh Grandmother, if people do not drown . . . "

The next three energy qualities are the quick ones:

Nervous or afraid/dabbing: Sudden or quick and light, at something, tic-like

Dab at paint with your fingers, then dab the paint on the wall as if you were holding a brush. Be the Sea Witch making a magic potion, dabbing the ingredients.

Agitated/flicking: Sudden or quick and light, anywhere in space

Flick an imaginary speck off your sleeve with your fingers, then flick at a fly with your right elbow and then with your left shoulder. Hold onto a partner's inside shoulder for support, and with agitation, flick your leg as if it were a fishtail.

Angry/slashing: Sudden or quick and strong, anywhere in space

Slash a sword. Slash a fishtail. Hold onto a partner's inside shoulder for support and angrily slash the water with your outside leg a few times.

Part 4: Improvisation (20 Minutes)

Leader: [Have the children refer to the improvisation guidelines in item 5 of their handout.]

- *Review your character statements and make sure that you have learned them in your own words. Feel free to say them in yet other ways, as long as you're giving the same message*

- *Say your character statements as you move to the mood or energy qualities, to see which fit the best, and to see if you still choose the same ones that you did for the vocal practice.*

- *Practice aligning your voice with your movements using the selected mood or energy quality. Remember that your nonverbal movements should send the same message as your voice; that is, they should convey the same mood or energy quality.*

Part 5: Presentations (30–45 Minutes)

After they practice, organize the children in the order of the items on the "Character Statement Selections" for presentations with the microphones. Keep the completed worksheets for the Part 3 workshop.

Practice Character Statement

"Grandmother, if people do not drown, do they live until the end of time?"

Character Statement Selections

Select from one of the following:

1. **The Grandmother to the Sea Princesses:**

   "At 15, you will have the opportunity to rise up above the water. You will see great ships, cities, and forests, and the people who live there."

2. **The Little Mermaid to Grandmother:**

   "It's my turn now; I can hardly wait to see the world above the ocean."

3. **The Little Mermaid to the Prince and then to herself:**

   "Oh, no, you mustn't die. I will hold your head above the water and carry you to safety."

4. **The Little Mermaid to Grandmother:**

   "I don't care about living for 300 years; I want to live forever; I want an immortal soul."

5. **The Sea Witch to The Little Mermaid:**

   "Ha, Ha, Ha; you're quite the fool. Your heart will break if he weds someone else, now won't it? Ha, Ha, Ha."

6. **The Prince to The Little Mermaid**

   "You are so sweet; you may stay with me forever."

7. **The Little Mermaid to herself:**

   "He has married someone else. I have given up everything for him and now I have no hope of an immortal soul."

8. **The Sisters to The Little Mermaid:**

   "The Witch has given us this knife for our beautiful long hair. It is for you; stab him; his dripping blood will restore your fishtail."

9. **The Little Mermaid to herself:**

   "I cannot kill him. I will throw myself into the sea and turn into foam."

10. **The Little Mermaid to the Daughters of the Air:**

    "I am not dead. I hear beautiful voices. Who calls me?"

11. **The Daughters of the Air to The Little Mermaid:**

    "We call you; we are the daughters of the air. You are joining us, to bring joy to those who suffer; in doing so, you will earn an immortal soul."

From *Stories on the Move: Integrating Literature and Movement with Children, Infants to Age 14* by Arlene Cohen. Illustrated by Andrea Fitcha McAllister. Westport, CT: Libraries Unlimited. Copyright © 2007.

Character Image Worksheet

1. Write your Character Statement Selection here:

2. Who is speaking here?

Where there is a choice, underline, circle, or highlight your choice:

3. Looks: My character looks like this: He or she is _____ feet tall, is large/small, fat/thin, posture is straight/crooked/curved has facial features that are rounded/sharp, has _____ colored hair, which is straight/curly/ frizzy, is wearing _____. Other comments about how my character looks:

Answer Number 4 after the Vocal Warm Up

4. Feels and Sounds: In my selection, my character sounds like he or she is (circle or underline one or more of the mood or energy qualities and write the part of the character's dialogue that fits that mood or energy):

Peaceful/floating: Sustained or slow and light, sense of rising up

Happy/gliding: Sustained or slow and light, level or even

Impatient/pressing: Sustained or slow and strong, forward direction

Nervous or afraid/dabbing: Sudden or quick and light, at something, tic like

Agitated/flicking: Sudden or quick and light, anywhere in space

Angry/slashing: Sudden or quick and strong, anywhere in space

5. Vocal Plus Movement Improvisation Guidelines

- Review your character statements and make sure that you have learned them in your own words. Feel free to say them in other ways, as long as they have the same meaning.

- Say your character statements as you move to the mood or energy qualities, to see which fit the best, and to see if you still choose the same ones that you did for the vocal practice.

- Practice aligning your voice with your movements using the selected mood or energy quality. Remember that your nonverbal movements should send the same message as your voice; that is, they should convey the same mood or energy quality.

Character Image Worksheet Sample

1. Write your Character Statement Selection here.

"Grandmother, if people do not drown, do they live until the end of time?"

2. Who is speaking here?

The Little Mermaid

Where there is a choice, underline, circle, or highlight your choice:

3. Looks: My character looks like this:

He or she is <u>5 feet 2 inches</u> tall, is large/<u>small,</u> fat/<u>thin,</u> posture is <u>straight</u>/crooked/<u>curved tail,</u> has facial features that are <u>rounded</u>/sharp, has <u>blond</u> colored hair, which is straight/<u>curly</u>/ frizzy, is wearing <u>flowers and jewelry</u>. Other comments about how your character looks: She has beautiful blue eyes, long lashes, rosy and clear skin.

Answer Number 4 after the Vocal Warm Up

4. Feels and Sounds: In my selection, my character sounds and moves like he or she is (circle or underline one or more of the energy qualities and write the part of the character's dialogue that fits that energy):

Peaceful/floating: Sustained or slow and light, sense of rising up
<u>Her energy is sustained and slow and light but it has no focus, as she says, "do they live until the end of time?" Her arms float up into the air</u>

Happy/gliding: Sustained or slow and light, level or even

Impatient/pressing: Sustained or slow and strong, forward direction
<u>The Little Mermaid's voice and movement is sustained or slow, but it is strong and has a forward direction, when she confronts her grandmother: The Little Mermaid presses her head and chest forward as she first confronts her grandmother with the question. "If people do not drown . . . "</u>

Nervous or afraid/dabbing: Sudden or quick and light, at something, tic like

Agitated/flicking: Sudden or quick and light, anywhere in space

Angry/slashing: Sudden or quick and strong, anywhere in space
<u>She slashes her tail here and there in anger after she finds out how difficult it is to become a human girl with legs.</u>
<u>After she stops speaking, her energy quality is sudden and has no focus, but instead of light, it is strong, as she slashes her tail back and forth to show her angry disappointment. The slashing can be shown by slashing the leg or arm slightly behind and to the side of the body.</u>

From *Stories on the Move: Integrating Literature and Movement with Children, Infants to Age 14* by Arlene Cohen. Illustrated by Andrea Fitcha McAllister. Westport, CT: Libraries Unlimited. Copyright © 2007.

Program 2: Moving Stories—Settings and Narration

Summary

In this second part of a three-part workshop, selected passages from a translation of "The Little Mermaid" for older children serve as the catalyst for learning how to align voice and movement to bring images of the narrated story settings to life. The program takes about two hours and builds on the activities of Part 1.

Program Preparation

Books

- Andersen, Hans Christian. "The Little Mermaid." In *Fairy Tales*. Translated by Tiina Nunnally. Edited and introduced by Jackie Wullschlager. New York: Viking, 2005. The Little Mermaid would gladly give up her lifespan of 300 years, if she could be a human girl and win the love of the Prince and an immortal soul.

Alternative Resources

- Andersen, Hans Christian. *The Little Mermaid*. Translated from the Danish by Anthea Bell. Illustrated by Lisbeth Zwerger. New York: Minedition/Penguin, 2004.

- Andersen, Hans Christian. *Little Mermaid and Ugly Duckling: Favorite Fairytales*. Illustrated by Gennady Spirin. San Francisco: Chronicle Books, c2001

Music

- "Malibu Surf," and other ocean sounds, from *Hush Little Baby: Soothing Sounds for Sleep*. Pacific Palisades, CA: Kids Music Factory, 2003.

Space Needs

- Two to three square feet of uncarpeted open space for each child

- Tables or desks and chairs for each child or seating on floor, with cushions and a hard surface on which to write

The environment should be free of interference noises such as those in a cafeteria.

Materials and Equipment

- CD and cassette player

- Percussion instruments: flat hand drum with drumstick or empty oatmeal box and large wooden spoon

- Microphones, preferably lavalieres, to rotate as children perform

- Handouts:
    - "Story Settings and Narration Selections" (at end of this section)
    - "Setting Image Worksheet" (at end of this section)
    - "Setting Image Worksheet Sample" (at end of this section)
- Pencils or pens for each child and a hard writing surface, such as a book or clipboard, if sitting on the floor

Before You Begin

- Make copies of the handouts for each child.
- Practice the activities.
- Gather and set up the equipment and materials.
- Copy this "Practice Setting Statement" (See handout at end of this section.):

    Under the water, there are no flowers to smell

    No birds to hear, no mountains and forests to see

Program

Introduction

Welcome everyone, to Part 2 of the "Moving Story" workshop. Today you will learn how to bring to life images of story settings with the alignment of your voice and movements. In this workshop you will portray a vivid setting image. To bring a setting to life, your audience must perceive through your voice and motion what your setting looks like, sounds like, and feels like, in the very moment you perform it. You immerse yourself in and have a vision or image of the setting so that your audience experiences the setting in the present moment. As we did in the first workshop, we will be using different qualities of mood or energy to align or coordinate our voice and motion. Would someone like to explain what I mean by aligning voice and movement? [Give them a chance to explain what they understood from Part 1 and what may need to be clarified.]

After you hear the story, you will be choosing from a selection of story settings said by the story narrator. You will convey the sense of your setting through how you speak and move as narrator. I will repeat the story. Today I'd like for you to focus on the narration about the settings. The *narrator* is the person who describes the setting, characters, and action in the story. The narrator does not usually take part in the story, as the characters do. It is important to distinguish between the narrator's voice and the character's voice. Most of the time the narrator's voice is your natural voice. There is a sense of objectivity in the narrator's voice, but you can vary the narrator's voice to create moods and give a hint of the character, place, or event that follows the narration. Today you will distinguish between dialogue and narration. As I tell the story, raise your hand when characters are speaking dialogue.

Story Presentation (10 Minutes)

Play "Malibu Surf" to set the mood. Stop the ocean sounds after the story introduction, for example, after the following story text: "her body ended in a fishtail." Reread or perform all or a portion of "The Little Mermaid" passages again. Read or perform enough that you know the children understand the difference between dialogue and narration.

Story Vocal and Movement Exercises

Part 1: Vocal Exercises (10 Minutes)

Leader: *Before each of the following, inhale deeply, and as you exhale make the sounds to warm up your voice, which start down in you abdomen, move up through your chest, through your vocal cords, and out through your mouth and nose. Make each sound three times, inhaling between each repetition:*

> *Inhale, exhale slowly, making the Ommmmmm sound*
>
> *Inhale, exhale: Ma Me Mi Mo Mu*
>
> *Inhale, exhale: Ta Te Ti To Tu*
>
> *Inhale, exhale wolf yowl: Ah Ouuuuu*
>
> *Inhale, exhale: NeNeNeNe*
>
> *Inhale, exhale witch laugh: Ha! Ha! Ha! Ha! Ha!*

Vocal Variations

Leader: *Now I want you to practice saying this setting selection in the different mood or energy qualities. Freely use whatever facial expressions or gestures come naturally with your voice.*

Here is a sample setting selection. We will try out the different mood or energy qualities with it. Let's memorize it first. [Hold up the enlarged "Practice Setting Statement" and have them repeat it three times:]

> *Under the water, there are no flowers to smell*
>
> *No birds to hear, no mountains and forests to see.*

Now, as I call out the mood or energy qualities, one by one, I want you to narrate this setting using each of the energy qualities:

- *Peaceful/floating: Sustained or slow and light, sense of rising up*

- *Happy/gliding: Sustained or slow and light, level or even*

- *Impatient/pressing: Sustained or slow and strong, forward direction*

- *Sad/dragging: Sustained or slow and strong with no direction*

- *Nervous or afraid/dabbing: Sudden or quick and light, at something, tic like*

- *Agitated/flicking: Sudden or quick and light, anywhere in space*

- *Angry/slashing: Sudden or quick and strong, anywhere in space*

Which variation(s) do you think work(s) best in this situation, considering the author's intention? [Give them time to answer and say why they chose that energy quality for the setting.]

Give the children the "Story Settings and Narration Selection" handout. Have them choose the setting that matches the number that they had in the "Character Statement Selections."

Part 3: Setting Appearance (20 Minutes)

Give children the " Setting Image Worksheet" handout and the sample worksheet handout.

- Review the sample and have the children fill in numbers 1 and 2.
- Have them practice and learn their setting statement, using the vocal variations.
- Have them answer number 3 on the "Setting Image Worksheet" handout.

Part 4: Movement Exercises (30 Minutes)

Leader: [Ask the children to do the following:]

1. *Walk clockwise around the circumference of the room a few times.* (Play the drum, accenting every count: 1-2-3-4-5-6-7-8; repeat several times at a moderate tempo).

2. *Spinal alignment: Stop.* [Demonstrate the following for them before they do it; be sure to bend your knees slightly as you roll down.] *Roll your upper body down from the top of your head, one vertebra at a time; bend your knees slightly as you roll down. Use all 8 counts to roll down.* [Count out loud: 1-2-3-4-5-6-7-8.] *Let your head hang forward heavily. Make hissing sounds as you hang your head for eight counts, dangling your arms and imagining water rolling off your back onto the floor. Slowly uncurl your body, one vertebra at a time from the base of your spine, up at eight counts.* [Count out loud: 1-2-3-4-5-6-7-8] *As before, your head should hang forward heavily until after you've uncurled your shoulders and neck.*

3. *Walk counterclockwise around the room a few times.* [Play the drum, accenting every count: 1-2-3-4-5-6-7-8; repeat several times at a moderate tempo.]

4. *Walk faster and faster and faster.* [Gradually increase the tempo, still accenting every count.]

5. *Now, begin to slow down, slower, slower, slower.* [Gradually decrease the tempo, accenting every count.] *Stop. Shake out your arms and legs.*

[Have everyone face you. They should remain spread around the room.] *We are going to square off now, so everyone will have adequate room to move in their personal space:*

1. *Raise your arms to the side, palms down, at shoulder level, parallel to the floor. Move apart so that you don't touch anyone else.*

2. *Make one one-quarter turn to the right and again raise your arms to the side at shoulder level, parallel to the floor. Again adjust your space so that you are not touching anyone.*

3. *Make another one-quarter turn to your right. You are opposite to where you started. Raise your arms as before.*

4. *Make another one-quarter turn to your right and raise your arms as before.*

5. *Make a final one-quarter turn to your right, facing front where you started.*

Now, I'm going to ask you to move the same part of your body to two different energy qualities:

- **Head and Neck**

    – *Peaceful/floating: Sustained or slow and light, sense of rising up*

      Now "float" your neck and head in a sustained and slow and light movement in any direction, like a balloon floating up into space.

    – *Happy/gliding: Sustained or slow and light, level or even*

      We will begin with the neck and head. Glide your head like a bird in flight for four counts to the right and then four counts to the left, twice.

- **Shoulders:** *Slowly press your shoulders forward twice and back twice. Repeat..*

    – *Impatient/Pressing: Sustained or slow and strong, forward direction*

    – *Sad/dragging: Sustained or slow and strong with no direction*

      Carry or drag a heavy weight, drooping your shoulders.

    – *Nervous or afraid/dabbing: Sudden or quick and light, at something, tic-like*

      Quickly and definitely shoot your shoulders up as if they were shooting arrows, twice.

- **Hands and Wrists**

    – *Agitated/flicking: Sudden or quick and light, anywhere in space*

      Flick your hands and wrists forward four times.

    – *Angry/slashing: Sudden or quick and strong, anywhere in space*

      Slash the air like fireworks exploding, with your right hand three times and then with your left hand three times.

The following is number 4 on your sample worksheets; you can refer to it as you create your setting interpretations. Please mirror me.

The Little Mermaid feels hindered, stuck in the ocean; it is like a prison to her. She wants to be a human girl, living above the sea, on land.

1. *Under the water, there are no flowers to smell. Pressing nose forward.*

    Movement: Press your nose up against the water to smell, and then move your head back and forth and lowering eyes, as if the narrator is saying "no, too bad."

2. *No birds to hear, no mountains and forests to see. Pressing ear out.*

    Movement: Press your ear up and out, then look out strongly against the water, and then move your head back and forth with eyes lowered, as if the narrator is saying, "no, to that too."

3. *The world of humans is much larger than the world under the water. Slashing tail all directions, shoulder pressing up and dropping.*

    Movement: Slash your tail back and forth, with your hips and your arm behind you, in all four directions, with your head looking up and down in all four directions, as if the narrator is saying, "no, there is nothing here for me." Press your shoulders forward and then drop them.

Part 5: Improvisation (20—30 Minutes)

Leader: *Follow the guidelines for improvisation in number 5 of your handout.*

- *Review your setting statements and make sure that you have learned them. You are encouraged to put them in your own words.*

- *Say your setting statement as you move to the mood or energy qualities, to see which ones fit the best, and to see if you still choose the same ones that you did for the vocal practice.*

- *Practice aligning your voice with your movements using the selected mood or energy quality. Remember that your nonverbal movements should send the same message as your voice; that is, they should convey the same mood or energy quality.*

- *Practice aligning your voice with your movements using the selected mood or energy quality.*

Part 6: Presentations (30—45 Minutes)

After the children practice, organize them in the order on the "Story Setting and Narrations Selection" handout for class presentations, using microphones. Keep the completed worksheets for the Part 3 workshop.

Practice Setting Statement

Under the water, there are no flowers to smell

No birds to hear, no mountains and forests to see.

From *Stories on the Move: Integrating Literature and Movement with Children, Infants to Age 14* by Arlene Cohen. Illustrated by Andrea Fitcha McAllister. Westport, CT: Libraries Unlimited. Copyright © 2007.

Story Settings and Narration Selection

Narration

Narration is a description of incidents or a course of events in a story. It does not contain dialogue but can contain intense emotion. How you use your voice and move makes it interesting. You can tell an entire story by narration, but dialogue makes it livelier. Narration is also exciting when you add descriptive sounds.

Select the same number that you selected on the "Character Statement Selection" handout.

1. **The Sea King's Palace**

   Beneath the ocean lies a beautiful palace.

   Its walls are made from coral reef

   Its roof is made of muscle shells

   Each shell opens and closes as the water flows through

2. **The Ocean with the Ship**

   Lightly as a bubble she rose up to the surface of the water

   The sun was setting, causing the clouds to turn rose and gold

   There before her was a ship with only one sail set for the sea was calm.

3. **The Stormy Ocean**

   Waves rose like huge dark mountains.

   The ship broke into pieces

   And the Prince was thrown out to sea

4. **Underwater Confinement**

   Under the water, there are no flowers to smell

   No birds to hear, no mountains and forests to see.

   The world of humans is much larger than the world under the water

5. **The Sea Witch Pathway and Home**

   No flowers grew there, no sea grass

   Only grey sand beds and grasping whirlpools

   And slimy shipwrecks

6. **The Prince's Castle**

   A marble staircase led to the castle

   It was a stately and luxurious palace

   With festivities and dancing girls

7. **The Marriage Vessel**

   On the ship was an exquisite marriage tent

   It was gold and purple and lined with velvet cushions.

   Brightly colored lamps lighted the dancers in the wedding party.

8. **The Ship's Railing**

   The massive ship glided smoothly upon the sea.

   Along the side of the ship was a railing upon which The Little Mermaid

   leaned and looked out to sea.

9. **The Wedding Tent**

   The prince and his lovely bride slept there

   inside the purple drapes, as the royal ship glided through

   the night sea on its return to the castle

10. **The Knife on the Ocean Waves and Foam**

    She went to the railing and threw the knife into the water.

    Then she threw herself into the water.

    The foam absorbed the body of The Little Mermaid.

11. **The Sky**

    The sky was filled with sunshine and beautiful transparent beings.

    The beings of the air floated upward.

    They were the daughters of the air

From *Stories on the Move: Integrating Literature and Movement with Children, Infants to Age 14* by Arlene Cohen. Illustrated by Andrea Fitcha McAllister. Westport, CT: Libraries Unlimited. Copyright © 2007.

Setting Image Worksheet

1. **My setting is called:**

2. **Looks: My setting looks like this:**

   The colors in my setting are

   The objects in my setting are

Answer Number 3 after the Vocal Warm Up

3. **Feels and Sounds:** In my selection, my narrator sounds like he or she is (circle or underline one or more of the mood or energy qualities and write the part of the narrator's description that fits that mood or energy):

   Peaceful/floating: Sustained or slow and light, sense of rising up

   Happy/gliding: Sustained or slow and light, level or even

From *Stories on the Move: Integrating Literature and Movement with Children, Infants to Age 14* by Arlene Cohen. Illustrated by Andrea Fitcha McAllister. Westport, CT: Libraries Unlimited. Copyright © 2007.

Impatient/pressing: Sustained or slow and strong, forward direction

Sad/dragging: Sustained or slow and weak, no direction

Nervous or afraid/dabbing: Sudden or quick and light, at something, tic-like

Agitated/flicking: Sudden or quick and light, anywhere in space

Angry/slashing: Sudden or quick and strong, anywhere in space

4. **Improvisation Guidelines**
    - Review your setting statements and make sure that you have learned them.
    - Say your setting statements as you move to the mood or energy qualities, to see which ones fit the best and to see if you still choose the same ones that you did for the vocal practice.
    - Practice aligning your voice with your movements using the selected mood or energy quality. Remember that your nonverbal movements should send the same message as your voice; that is, they should convey the same mood or energy quality.
    - Practice aligning your voice with your movements using the selected mood or energy quality.

Setting Image Worksheet Sample

1. **My setting is called:**

    Underwater Confinement

2. **Looks: My setting looks like this:**

The colors in my setting are

Blue, green, gold primarily

The objects in my setting are

The underwater palace, fish, plants, sea animals

A prison: To The Little Mermaid, the ocean has become a place without interesting things to see, hear, or smell. She sees it as a place of limited possibilities; she feels imprisoned there. Her perception of her life distorts the setting. The narrator must convey this distortion.

 From *Stories on the Move: Integrating Literature and Movement with Children, Infants to Age 14* by Arlene Cohen. Illustrated by Andrea Fitcha McAllister. Westport, CT: Libraries Unlimited. Copyright © 2007.

3. Feels and Sounds:

In my selection my narrator sounds and moves like he or she is (circle or underline one or more of the energy qualities and write the part of the passage that goes with it; see sample answers.

Peaceful/floating: Sustained or slow and light with sense of rising up

Happy/gliding: Sustained or slow and light, level or even

Impatient/pressing: Sustained or slow and strong, forward direction
Under the water, there are no flowers to smell
Pressing nose up against water to smell, and then head back and forth and low-
    ering eyes, as if narrator is saying *"no, too bad"*
No birds to hear, no mountains and forests to see.
Pressing ear up and out and then looking out strongly against water, and then head
    back and forth and eyes lowered, as if narrator is saying, *"no, to that too."*

Sad/dragging: Sustained or slow and weak, no direction

Nervous or afraid/dabbing: Sudden or quick and light, at something, tic-like

Agitated/flicking: Sudden or quick and light, anywhere in space

Angry/slashing: Sudden or quick and strong, anywhere in space The world of
    humans is much larger than the world under the water
    Slashing of tail back and forth, with leg as a tail as if the narrator is saying,
    "no, there is nothing here for The Little Mermaid." Shoulders press forward
    and then drop.

From *Stories on the Move: Integrating Literature and Movement with Children, Infants to Age 14* by Arlene Cohen. Illustrated by Andrea Fitcha McAllister. Westport, CT: Libraries Unlimited. Copyright © 2007.

Program 3: Moving Stories—Events

Summary

In this third part of a three-part workshop, event images of "The Little Mermaid" for older children serve as the catalyst for learning how to use voice and movement to bring to life images of the story events. The program takes about two hours and builds on the activities in Parts 1 and 2. Children should have the completed worksheets from Parts 1 and 2 to recall what they did previously for the improvisations. They will combine their previous improvisations in this event program.

Program Preparation

Space Needs

- Two to three square feet of uncarpeted open space for each child
- Tables or desks and chairs for each child or seating on the floor, with cushions and a hard surface on which to write.

The environment should be free of interference noises such as those in a cafeteria.

Materials and Equipment

- CD and cassette player
- Percussion instruments: flat hand drum with drumstick or empty oatmeal box and large wooden spoon
- Microphones, preferably lavalieres, to rotate as children perform
- Pencils or pens and paper for each child and a hard writing surface, such as a book or clipboard, if sitting on the floor
- Handouts
    - "Event Selections" (at end of this section)
    - "Story Structure" (at end of this chapter)
    - handouts completed in Parts 1 and 2

Before You Begin

- Make copies of handouts for each child.
- Gather and set up the equipment and materials.
- Study and practice the activities in the program.

Program

Introduction

> Welcome everyone, to Part 3 of the "Moving Story" experience. Today you will learn how to bring images of story events to life through the alignment of your voice and movements. As with character and setting, your audience will perceive through your voice and motions what your event looks like, sounds like, and feels like, in the very moment you perform it. You immerse yourself in and have a vision of the event so that your audience experiences the event in the present moment. The events that you will interpret today are a combination of the character's dialogue and the narrator's description of the setting in which the dialogue takes place, that is, what you have already been practicing. Today we will put them together. You will see the event both subjectively and objectively. What the character says is subjective. What the narrator says is objective, but as you've learned, what the narrator says can be colored by the character's perception of the circumstance. So, even though The Little Mermaid's home under the sea is still beautiful, she doesn't think so after she sees life above the sea. [Give children the "Story Structure" handout and review it with them.]

Leader: *You have heard the story twice. Let's recall the structure of "The Little Mermaid" story:*

- *What characters and setting are introduced in the introduction?*
- *What was the initial incident or event?*
- *What are the events following the initial event?*
- *What is the high point?*
- *What is the conclusion?*

See how much they can recall before giving them the "Event Selections" handout. The initial incident, high point, and conclusion are noted.

Story Vocal and Movement Exercises

Part 1: Vocal Exercises (5 Minutes)

Leader: *Before each of the following, inhale deeply, and as you exhale make the sounds to warm up your voice, which start down in you abdomen, move up through your chest, through your vocal cords, and out through your mouth and nose. Makey each sound three times, inhaling between each repetition:*

> *Inhale, exhale slowly, making the Ommmmmm sound*
>
> *Inhale, exhale: Ma Me Mi Mo Mu*

Inhale, exhale: Ta Te Ti To Tu

Inhale, exhale wolf yowl: Ah Ouuuuu

Inhale, exhale: NeNeNeNe

Inhale, exhale witch laugh: Ha! Ha! Ha! Ha! Ha!

Part 2: Movement Exercises (30 Minutes)

Have children choose the event number that coincides with their character and setting selections. All events should be chosen.

Leader:

1. *Walk clockwise around the circumference of the room a few times.* [Play the drum, accenting every count: 1-2-3-4-5-6-7-8; repeat several times at a moderate tempo.]

2. *Spinal alignment: Stop.* [Demonstrate the following for them before they do it; be sure to bend your knees slightly as you roll down.] *Roll your upper body down from the top of your head, one vertebra at a time; bend your knees slightly as you roll down. Use all 8 counts to roll down.* [Count out loud: 1-2-3-4-5-6-7-8.] *Let your head hang forward heavily. Make hissing sounds as you hang your head forward for eight counts, dangling your arms and imagining water rolling off your back onto the floor. Slowly uncurl your body, one vertebra at a time from the base of your spine, up at eight counts.* [Count out loud: 1-2-3-4-5-6-7-8.] *As before, your head should hang forward heavily until after you've uncurled your shoulders and neck.*

3. *Walk counterclockwise around the room a few times.* [Play the drum, accenting every count: 1-2-3-4-5-6-7-8; repeat several times at a moderate tempo.]

4. *Walk faster and faster and faster.* [Gradually increase the tempo, still accenting every count.]

5. *Now, begin to slow down, slower, slower, slower.* [Gradually decrease the tempo, accenting every count.] *Stop. Shake out your arms and legs.*

[Have everyone face you. They should remain spread around the room.] *We are going to square off now, so everyone will have adequate room to move in their personal space:*

1. *Raise your arms to the side, palms down, at shoulder level, parallel to the floor. Move apart so that you don't touch anyone else.*

2. *Make one one-quarter turn to the right and again raise your arms to the side at shoulder level, parallel to the floor. Again adjust your space so that you are not touching anyone.*

3. *Make another one-quarter turn to your right. You are opposite to where you started. Raise your arms as before.*

4. *Make another one-quarter turn to your right and raise your arms as before.*

5. *Make a final one-quarter turn to your right, facing front where you started.*

Again, as in the previous workshop, I'm going to ask you to move the same part of your body to two different energy qualities. Today we are adding directions. Let your eyes lead your movement; look in the direction that you are going.

- **Peaceful/floating: Sustained or slow and light, sense of rising up**

    "Float" your head off your shoulders and let it settle two times, in four counts. Now float your head to the right corner of the room and let it settle, then float it to the left corner of the room and let it settle.

The Floating Head—Three Directions.

- **Happy/gliding: Sustained or slow and light, level or even**

    Turn your head and glide it for four counts to the right and then four counts to the left, and then four counts to the front and four counts straight back; keep your head level.

- **Impatient/pressing: Sustained or slow and strong, forward direction**

    Press your shoulders forward two times and back two times, twice. Then press your upper body from the waist to the side, with the movement starting in the right and then the left shoulder.

- **Sad/dragging: Sustained or slow and strong with no direction**

    Droop your shoulders, release them. and repeat several times

- *Nervous or afraid/dabbing: Sudden or quick and light, at something, tic like*

  Dab your shoulders nervously, like shaking, several times.

- *Agitated/flicking: Sudden or quick and light, anywhere in space*

  Flick your hand and wrist forward four times. Now flick them backward behind you four times.

- *Angry/slashing: Sudden or quick and strong, anywhere in space*

  Slash the air with your right arm to your right side three times and then to your left side with your left arm. Then slash with your right arm to the left side three times and with the left arm to your right side three times.

For the last part of our warm-up we are going to combine these energy qualities to form a movement composition. Without stopping, I would like you to do the following sequences, as I call them out one by one:

1. *Glide, float, and explode your right arm to the front and to the side; now glide, float, and explode your left arm to the front and to the side.*

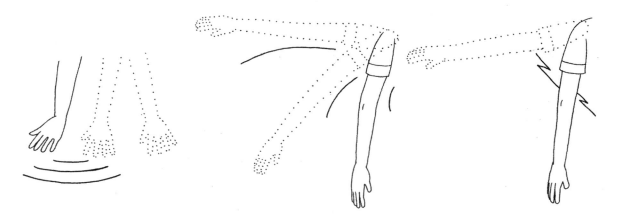

Gliding, Floating, and Exploding Arm.

2. *Float your right arm, flick your right hand, and explode your right hip to the right side; now float your left arm, flick your left hand, and explode your left hip to the left side.*

3. *Explode your right arm, shoot out your right foot, point your right index finger, and glide your head to the right and back to center; now explode your left arm, shoot out your left foot, point your left index finger, and glide your head to the left and back to center. Let your head float up in the air and press your shoulders down. Let your head float back to your neck. Roll your head down to the floor, dropping your back vertebra by vertebra, hanging heavily. Exhale deeply, letting your head hang heavier. Now slowly roll up, one vertebra at a time. Shrug your shoulders and shake out your body.*

Part 3: Improvisation (30 Minutes)

Leader: *Here is a sample moving story composition, including character and narration, in which both movement and speech are aligned through the use of the energy qualities. It is a combination of what we did in the first two workshops.*

"Grandmother, if people do not drown, do they live"

> *The Little Mermaid <u>presses her head and body forward</u> as she confronts her grandmother with this question.*

"until the end of time?"

> *Her <u>arms float up into the air like a balloon</u> as she says, "until the end of time?"*

Under the water, there are no flowers to smell

> *She presses her nose up against the water to smell and then glides her head back and forth and lowers her eyes, as if the narrator is saying "no, too bad."*

No birds to hear, no mountains and forests to see.

> *She presses her ear up and out, then looks out strongly against the water, and then glides her head back and forth with eyes lowered, as if the narrator is saying, "no, to that too."*

The world of humans is much larger than the world under the water

> *She <u>explosively slashes her tail back and forth</u> to show her anger. The slashing can be shown by slashing the leg or arm slightly behind and to the side of the body, or with her hips as a tail and her arm behind and to the side, in all four directions, with her head looking up and down in all four directions, as if the narrator is saying, "no, there is nothing here for me." Her shoulders press forward and then drop.*

Now you are going to combine your character and setting improvisation to form a "Moving Story" event composition. Review your Character and Setting Worksheets and practice combining them. Align your voice and movements so they sound and move as one event image. You may add dialogue and narration, if you wish. Whatever you add needs to fit in with your part and the whole story.

Part 4: Presentations (30—45 Minutes)

After the children practice, organize them in the order shown on the Event Selections handout for class presentations with microphones.

Event Selections

Select the passage that corresponds with your previous number. Read and learn the whole passage, even if there is another character mentioned or speaking. As storytellers, you play all the parts and the narration.

1. **Initial Incident: The Little Mermaid finds out that she will be able to observe life on land when she is 15.**

   Beneath the ocean lies a beautiful palace.

   Its walls are made from coral reef

   Its roof is made of muscle shells

   Each shell opens and closes as the water flows through

   Grandmother: "At 15, you will have the opportunity to rise up above the water. You will see great ships, cities, and forests, and the people who live there."

2. **The Little Mermaid turns 15 and rises above the water.**

   Little Mermaid: "It's my turn now; I can hardly wait to see the world above the ocean."

   Lightly as a bubble she rose up to the surface of the water

   The sun was setting, causing the clouds to turn rose and gold

   There before her was a ship with only one sail set for the sea was calm.

3. **The Little Mermaid sees and rescues the Prince from a shipwreck.**

   Waves rose like huge dark mountains.

   The ship broke into pieces

   And Prince was thrown out to sea.

   Little Mermaid: "Oh, no, you mustn't die. I will hold your head above the water and carry you to safety."

   "Who is that girl; he thinks she saved him; but I did."

4. **The Little Mermaid wants to be a human girl.**

   Little Mermaid: "I don't care about living for 300 years; I want to live forever; I want an immortal soul."

   Under the water, there are no flowers to smell

   No birds to hear, no mountains and forests to see.

   The world of humans is much larger than the world under the water.

5. **The Little Mermaid seeks "legs" from the Sea Witch.**

   No flowers grew there, no sea grass

   Only grey sand beds and grasping whirlpools

   And slimy shipwrecks

Sea Witch: "I know why you're here. Ha, Ha, Ha; you're quite the fool. Your heart will break if he weds someone else, now won't it? Ha, Ha, Ha. Drink this, if you want a pair of human legs; it is made from my blood."

6. **The Prince finds The Little Mermaid as a human girl on land near the palace.**

> A marble staircase led to the castle
>
> It was a stately and luxurious palace
>
> with festivities and dancing girls.
>
> Prince: "You are so sweet; you may stay with me forever."

7. **The Prince weds another.**

> On the ship was an exquisite marriage tent
>
> It was gold and purple and lined with velvet cushions.
>
> Brightly colored lamps lighted the dancers in the wedding party.
>
> Little Mermaid: "He has married someone else. I have given up everything for him and now I have no hope of an immortal soul."

8. **The sisters bring a knife.**

> The massive ship glided smoothly upon the sea.
>
> Along the side of the ship was a railing upon which The Little Mermaid
>
> leaned and looked out to sea.
>
> Sisters: "The witch has given us this knife for our beautiful long hair. It is for you; stab him; his dripping blood will restore your fishtail."

9. **High Point: The Little Mermaid does not kill the Prince.**

> The prince and his lovely bride slept there
>
> inside the purple drapes, as the royal ship glided through
>
> the night sea on its return to the castle.
>
> Little Mermaid: "I cannot kill him. I will throw myself into the sea and turn into foam."

10. **The Little Mermaid throws the knife and herself into the ocean.**

> She went to the railing and threw the knife into the water. Then she threw herself into the water. The foam absorbed the body of The Little Mermaid.
>
> "I am not dead. I hear beautiful voices. Who calls me?"

11. **Conclusion: The Daughters of the Air.**

> The sky was filled with sunshine and beautiful transparent beings.
>
> The beings of the air floated upward.
>
> They were the daughters of the air.
>
> "We call you; we are the daughters of the air. You are joining us, to bring joy to those who suffer and in doing so you will earn an immortal soul."

Program 4: Moving Fables—Selection, Analysis, and Rehearsal

Summary

In "Moving Fables" Part 1 the children select, visualize, analyze, and edit a fable and begin rehearsing. In Program 4 they align voice and movement and refine what they've learned for a performance for other children, families, the school, the library, or the community. It is highly recommended that additional workshops before and after Program 5 be scheduled, as well as a dress rehearsal. These additional workshops would be for performance coaching on the entire fable and costume preparation using poster paper or other materials. Costumes can be simply ears and tales of the animals in the fables. Storytellers perform all the characters, setting, objects, and events in a story. They may adapt the fable by adding to or changing the setting, characters, and events; they may also add an introduction and conclusion. Part 1 lasts about two and a half to three hours. The two-part "Moving Fables" workshop can be done separately but does build on the three "Moving Stories" programs for those who are new to performing.

Program Preparation

Books

- Pinkney, Jerry. "The North Wind and the Sun." In *Aesop's Fables*. New York: SeaStar Books, 2000. Workshop example. The North Wind and the Sun argue about who has the most strength. The Sun proves, through using gentle persuasion, that it does. This book is an excellent source for the children's fable selection and adaptation.

Other Source of Fables

- Morpurgo, Michael. *The McElderry Book of Aesop's Fables*. Illustrations by Emma Chichester Clark. New York: Margaret K. McElderry Books, 2005. These fables are written in story form with an introduction, dialogue, a sequence of events, and a conclusion. Good for those who don't want to edit; but they are lengthier than the standard fable. It also contains a version of "The North Wind and the Sun."

Space Needs

- Two to three square feet of uncarpeted open space for each child,

The environment should be free of interference noises such as those in a cafeteria.

Materials and Equipment

- Tables or desks and chairs on one side for each child or seating on floor, with cushions and a hard surface on which to write

- Microphone, preferably lavaliere for ease of movement (for a performance for a larger audience, two or three lavaliere microphones to put on and take off performers as they perform)
- Pencils or pens for each child
- Notebook paper for creating changes or additions to setting, characters, or events
- Handouts:
    - "Story Structure" (at end of this chapter)
    - "Fable Analysis Worksheet" (at end of this section)
    - "Fable Story Form" (at end of this section)
    - "Trigger Method of Learning a Fable" (at end of this section)

Before You Begin

- Make a list of titles and two copies of fables from one or more of the books listed above. Give each child a copy and save a master copy. It is recommended that the children select their fables a few days before the workshop, to save time.
- Gather all materials.
- Make copies of all handouts (four forms for each child).
- Review the program and handout contents.
- Read or learn the fable, "The North Wind and the Sun" and the edits included in this program. Add or change anything else that you wish. If you have not told a story before and wish to perform the fable, see the "Trigger Method for Learning a Story (Group Leader)" handout at the end of this chapter.

Program

Introduction

> Welcome to Part 1 of the "Moving Fables" workshop. Today you will hear, select, analyze, and edit a fable. [Give children the "Story Structure: handout.]
>
> *Fables* are condensed stories, are composed of images like a story, and have an important message. Frequently they do not have a distinct introduction or conclusion, or many events, but they do have a setting and characters. Like stories, fables usually have both narration and dialogue. *Narration* is the act of giving an account *describing* incidents or a course of events. It does not contain dialogue but can contain intense emotion. How you use your voice and how you move make it interesting. One can perform an entire fable by narration, but fables are more interesting when they contain dialogue.

> Here is how a full traditional story is structured; you may refer to your handout:
>
> - Introduction, in which the characters and setting are introduced
>
> - Initial incident, an event that triggers the rest of the action in the story
>
> - Plot, a sequence of events: A leads to B, leads to C, etc.
>
> - High point, the most intense part of the story
>
> - Conclusion, a resolution
>
> *Dialogue* is what characters say out loud to themselves or another character in a story. What the characters do and say in a fable mirrors how humans think, act, and interact with each other. Fables teach a lesson about life, which is usually stated at the end of the story, in the story conclusion.
>
> As I read [or perform] the following fable, see if you can identify a setting, characters, events, an introduction, an initial incident, a high point, and a conclusion or an important lesson. Also look for dialogue and narration in the fable.

Fable Presentation (5 Minutes)

Read or perform the fable "The North Wind and the Sun."

Fable Exercises

Part 1: Presented Fable Analysis (25 Minutes)

Give children an opportunity to respond to the questions or instructions below and confirm the answers:

Leader: *Name the settings and objects in this fable.*

Answer: The sky, a sidewalk, a tree, blasts of frigid air, cloak, hat, warm beams of light.

Leader: *Is there a character(s) in this fable?*

Answer: North Wind, Sun, Man.

Leader: *Is there narration in this fable? Is there dialogue? Who speaks to whom?*

Answer: Yes, both, mostly dialogue.

Leader: *What are the events in this story?*

Answer: The North Wind brags, the Sun challenges the North Wind. Each takes a turn to show strength in getting the man to remove his cloak. The Sun is victorious.

Leader: *Is there a high point?*

Answer: When the sunbeams cause the man to remove his cloak.

Leader: *Is there a conclusion, a message?*

Answer: The Sun was successful because it used gentle persuasion instead of force.

Leader: *I have added an introduction to my fable: "One day the North Wind and the Sun got into an argument." I also added a conclusion: "The North Wind had to agree that the sun was the irresistible one."* [If not previously selected, let the children select fables or give them fables to work on. Give them the "Fable Story Form" handout. Review the handout and have them fill it in. Ask them to read their fable a couple of times and then ask them to add an introduction and conclusion, if they are not already part of the fable.]

Part 2: Fable Selection (30–40 Minutes)

If possible, have the children select their fable a few days before the workshop, to save time. Have them add an introduction and a conclusion to their fable, if they want to do so. Also, they may change characters, setting, and events. Encourage them to change narration to dialogue or add dialogue to the narration.

Part 3: Visualization (20 Minutes)

Have the children close their eyes and listen to what you say. Give them plenty of time between each visualization before going on to the next one.

Leader: *While keeping your eyes closed, I want you to imagine how your characters look . . . how your settings look . . . how the events look . . . . Now I want you to imagine how your characters might feel inside . . . how your settings and the objects in your settings might feel when you touch them. Now I want you to imagine how your characters sound . . . can you hear any sounds in the now settings? Last, please imagine how your characters and objects move in your fable.*

Part 4: Selected Fable Analysis (30 Minutes)

Give the children and the "Fable Analysis Worksheet" handout and review it with them. Then have them fill in the responses, based on their edited version and their visualization.

Part 5: Rehearsal (30–45 Minutes)

Leader: *Now I'd like you rehearse your fable, adding and reflecting facial expressions, moods, and gestures suggested by the text.* [Give them the "Trigger Method of Learning a Fable" handout and go through it step by step with them, as they complete the steps.]

Each child presents what he or she has practiced to the rest of the group, using a microphone. Ask the children to rehearse their fable before Workshop 2, or provide additional workshops for rehearsal and coaching. Ask them to bring their costumes for Workshop 2, or make costumes in an additional workshop.

Suggestion: Make copies of or keep their completed handouts in case participants forget to bring them to Program 5.

Fable Story Form

Possible Introductions:

When and Where: Circle one or write your own introduction

Once upon a time, In the forest/other location,

Possible Conclusions:

And so as you can see **(and state the moral in your own words or just tell what lesson the fable taught).**

Fable Analysis Worksheet

1. Describe the characters in your fable: how do they look, sound, and move?

2. Describe the settings or objects in your fable: how do they look, sound, and move?

3. If there is an introduction in your fable? Who, where, and what is introduced?

4. **Events list:** Write a few words to trigger each fable event in your mind. The introduction precedes your first incident. Your first incident is your initial incident; the high point comes just before the conclusion. List your events below; you may have more or less than the numbers on this list, so renumber if necessary. Usually one paragraph is equal to one event. Remember that the initial incident is what gets the story rolling; one thing causes the next from there on.

1. **Initial incident:**

2.

3.

4.

5. **High point:**

6. **Conclusion/lesson or moral:**

Trigger Method of Learning a Fable

1. **Highlight the key words (nouns, verbs) and phrases; ignore the articles and prepositions.** The key words will trigger your memory of the sentence. It is not necessary to learn or memorize a sentence word-for-word; it sounds much better if you put the sentence in your own words. Your own words can change every time you tell the story, as long as the essence of the sentence is preserved. This process gives spontaneity to your performance and makes the audience believe what you are telling them. It is just like telling a friend about an experience that you had. The audience is a group of friends enjoying your reliving of your experience; in this case it happens to be a story that you've rehearsed.

2. **Make an events list of the story and note the introduction, initial incident, high point, and conclusion** (see the "Story Structure: handout at the end of this chapter). If you filled out the "Fable Analysis Worksheet for Workshop 1," you will find your events list under number 4. The events list is short list of two or three words that will trigger your memory of each event, as well as the introduction and conclusion. Memorize the short list so that you know the sequence of events.

3. **Divide the fable into two or three parts.** Learn one part completely before going on to the next part, by doing the following:

    a. Reread the first part out loud to yourself a few times.

    b. Read only the highlighted words out loud to yourself a few times.

    c. Tell Part 1, with the full text in view, and when necessary glance at the highlighted words.

    d. Tell Part 1 using the events list, without the full text in view.

    e. Go back and look at the full text of Part 1 to see what you may have missed.

    f. Tell Part 1 without using anything: Do not look at the events list, highlighted words, or full text.

    g. Go back and add vocal intonations, facial expressions, gestures, and movements that send the same message as the text.

    h. Do the same with Parts 2 and 3. Then right away practice your first and second and third parts together.

Program 5: Moving Fables—Improvisation and Performance

Summary

In this program the children learn and practice vocal and movement performance techniques to add to the fable text that they have learned. This program builds on the first part of "Moving Fables" (Program 4). Program 5 lasts two to two and a half hours, in preparation for a performance. It is recommended that more sessions be scheduled for coaching, rehearsal, and costume making.

Program Preparation

Space Needs

- Two to three square feet of uncarpeted open space for each child

The environment should be free of interference noises such as those in a cafeteria.

Materials and Equipment

- Microphone, preferably lavaliere for ease of movement (for performance for a larger audience, two or three lavaliere microphones to put on and take off performers as they perform)
- Handouts:
    - "Moods or Energy Qualities" (at end of this chapter)
    - Completed "Fable Analysis Worksheet" for Program 4
- Pens or pencils for each child
- Tables or desks and chairs on one side for each child or seating on floor, with cushions and a hard surface on which to write

Before You Begin

- Review and practice the content of the program.
- Gather the materials and set up the microphones.
- Copy the handouts, one of each for each child.

Program

Introduction

> Welcome to the second part of the "Moving Fable" workshop. Today you will learn how to bring the fable images to life by aligning your voice and movements, by conveying the same message in how you speak and how you move. For those who have had the "Moving Stories" workshops, this is a refresher.

Fable Vocal and Movement Exercises

Part 1: Vocal Exercises (15 Minutes)

Leader: *Say each of the following two times. On the second time, project your voice across the room:*

Inhale, exhale slowly, making the Ommmmmm sound

Inhale, exhale: Ma Me Mi Mo Mu

Inhale, exhale: Ta Te Ti To Tu

Inhale, exhale wolf yowl: Ah Ouuuuu

Inhale, exhale: NeNeNeNe

Inhale, exhale witch laugh: Ha! Ha! Ha! Ha! Ha!

Part 2: Moods and Energy Qualities (20–30 Minutes)

Make sure the children have their completed worksheets from Program 4.

Leader: *Referring to number 4, your list of events, on your completed "Fable Analysis Worksheet," assign one of the mood or energy qualities to each event and the characters in that event.* [Give them the "Moods or Energy Qualities" handout (at end of this chapter) and review it with them.] *They are as follows:*

- *Peaceful/floating: Sustained or slow and light, sense of rising up*

- *Happy/gliding: Sustained or slow and light, level or even*

- *Impatient/pressing: Sustained or slow and strong, forward direction*

- *Sad/dragging: Sustained or slow and strong with no direction*

- *Nervous or afraid/dabbing: Sudden or quick and light, at something, tic like*

- *Agitated/flicking: Sudden or quick and light, anywhere in space*

- *Angry/slashing: Sudden or quick and strong, anywhere in space*

Have them circle or underline the energy qualities that apply to each part of their fable on the "Moods or Energy Qualities" handout and then notate those moods or energies next to the related event (number 4) on their worksheet from the previous workshop.

Part 3: Movement Exercises (15 Minutes)

Leader: [Ask the children to do the following:]

1. *Walk clockwise around the circumference of the room a few times.* [Play the drum, accenting every count: 1-2-3-4-5-6-7-8; repeat several times at a moderate tempo.]

2. *Spinal alignment: Stop.* [Demonstrate the following for them before they do it; be sure to bend your knees slightly as you roll down.] *Roll your upper body down from the top of your head, one vertebra at a time; bend your knees slightly as you roll down. Use all 8 counts to roll down.* [Count out loud: 1-2-3-4-5-6-7-8.] *Let your head hang forward heavily. Make hissing sounds as you hang your head forward for eight counts, dangling your arms and imagining water rolling off your back onto the floor. Slowly uncurl your body, one vertebra at a time from the base of your spine, up at eight counts.* [Count out loud: 1-2-3-4-5-6-7-8.] *As before, your head should hang forward heavily until after you've uncurled your shoulders and neck.*

3. *Walk counterclockwise around the room a few times.* [Play the drum, accenting every count: 1-2-3-4-5-6-7-8; repeat several times at a moderate tempo.]

4. *Walk faster and faster and faster.* [Gradually increase the tempo, still accenting every count.]

5. *Now, begin to slow down, slower, slower, slower.* [Gradually decrease the tempo, accenting every count.] *Stop. Shake out your arms and legs.*

Part 4: Improvisation (30 Minutes)

Leader: *Please practice your movements, facial expressions, and gestures for the fable. Remember that your movements must mirror the text and reinforce the text message or image. Please refer to and use the mood or energy qualities that you've noted on your events list, number 4 of your worksheet.*

Part 5: Rehearsals (35–45 Minutes)

Have the children perform for the rest of the group with a microphone. Avoid performing in rooms with poor acoustics, such as cafeterias. Allow time to give them feedback, if you plan a dress rehearsal and final performance in the near future. I would also suggest that you add additional workshops before the dress rehearsal to coach each child for about 10 minutes, while the others are rehearsing by performing for another child or are making costumes.

Story Structure

A **story structure** is the framework of a story. It contains the following:

- **Introduction.** The opening of a story, in which the characters and setting are introduced.

- **Initial incident.** The first story event that sets off the other events; it triggers the rest of the action in the story.

- **Sequence of events.** The order of events that makes up the plot of the story: A leads to B, leads to C, etc.

- **High point.** The point that A, B, C, etc., lead to; it is the most intense part of the story.

- **Conclusion.** The resolution of the story and whatever issue was triggered by the initial incident.

Moods or Energy Qualities

1. **Peaceful/floating:** Sustained or slow and light, sense of rising up

2. **Happy/gliding:** Sustained or slow and light, level or even

3. **Impatient/pressing:** Sustained or slow and strong, forward direction

4. **Sad/dragging:** Sustained or slow and strong with no direction

5. **Nervous or afraid/dabbing:** Sudden or quick and light, at something, tic like

6. **Agitated/flicking:** Sudden or quick and light, anywhere in space

7. **Angry/slashing:** Sudden or quick and strong, anywhere in space

Trigger Method of Learning a Story (Group Leader)

1. **Highlight the key words (nouns, verbs) and phrases; ignore the articles, and prepositions.** The key words will trigger your memory of the sentence. It is not necessary to learn or memorize a sentence word-for-word; it sounds much better if you put the sentence in your own words. Your own words can change every time you tell the story, as long as the essence of the sentence is preserved. This process gives spontaneity to your performance and makes the audience believe what you are telling them. It is just like telling a friend about an experience that you've had. The audience is a group of friends enjoying your reliving of your experience; in this case it happens to be a story that you've rehearsed.

2. **Make an events list of the story and note the introduction, initial incident, high point, and conclusion** (see "Story Structure" handout, above). The events list is a short list of two or three words that trigger your memory of each event as well as the introduction and conclusion. Memorize the short list so that you know the sequence of events.

3. **Divide your the story into three parts;** learn one part completely before going onto the next part, by doing the following:

    a. Reread the first part out loud to yourself a few times.

    b. Read only the highlighted words out loud to yourself a few times.

    c. Tell Part 1 with the full text in view, and when necessary glance at the highlighted words.

    d. Tell Part 1 from the events list, without the full text in view.

    e. Go back and look at the full text of Part 1 to see what you may have missed.

    f. Tell Part 1 without using anything: Do not look at the events list, highlighted words, or full text.

    g. Do the same with Part 2. Then right away practice your first and seconds part together.

    h. Practice the second part. Then right away practice your first and second part together.

    i. Practice the third part. Then practice right away, parts 1, 2, and 3 together.

    j. Go back and add vocal intonations, facial expressions, gestures, and movement that sends the same message as the text.

Appendix A:
Dancing Parts of Speech

Children learn movement concepts and increase their vocabulary at the same time by putting the following words into action.

Dancing Verbs

gallop	hop	leap
roll	run	tiptoe
walk	bend forward	bend to the side
float	glide	press
punch	shake	flick
slash	spin	stretch
turn	twist	wiggle

Dancing Prepositions (Space, Directions, Levels)

high/low	over/under	out/in
forward/backward	right/left around	left/around right
side right/left	right/left/straight	curved
zigzag	angular	up/down

Dancing Adjectives (Shapes)

large/small	wide/narrow
straight/crooked/curved	round/pointed
smooth/sharp	fat thin
symmetrical/asymmetrical	

Dancing Adverbs (Movement Qualities)

much/little	heavy/light
strong/soft	tight/loose
explosive/smooth	surging/profusely

211

Appendix B:
Glossary of Dance Methods

Choreographed dance. A composed dance with defined movement for children to imitate.

Free form movement. Activity in which everyone spontaneously makes up movements to music.

Guided movement. Activity in which images suggest movement for children to create.

Imitative movement. Activity in which children mirror what a leader does as the music plays.

Improvisation. Activity in which children design their own movement and/or dialogue and narration.

References and Suggested Readings

References

American Academy of Pediatrics. 1998. *Caring for Your Baby and Young Child: Birth to Age 5.* New York: Bantam.

Benton, Michael. 1979. "Children's Responses to Stories." *Children's Literature in Education* 10:2, 72.

Bybee, R. W. and R. B. Sund. 1982. *Piaget for Educators.* 2d ed. Columbus, OH: Charles Merrill.

Dimondstein, Geraldine. 1971. *Children Dance in the Classroom.* New York: Macmillan, 10.

Fleming, Gladys Andrews. 1973. *Children's Dance.* Washington, DC: American Association for Health, Physical Education and Recreation, 41.

Laban, Rudolf. 1975. *Modern Educational Dance.* London: Macdonald and Evans, 49.

Landalf, Helen, and Pamela Gerke. 1996. *Movement Stories: For Young Children Ages 3–6,* Lyme, NH: Smith and Kraus, 1.

Shore, Rima. 1997. *Rethinking the Brain: New Insights into Early Development.* New York: Families and Work Institute.

Suggested Readings

Allstrom, Elizabeth. *Let's Play a Story.* New York: Friendship Press, [1957].

American Academy of Pediatrics. *Caring for Your Baby and Young Child: Birth to Age 5.* New York: Bantam, 1998.

Barlin, Anne Lief. *Teaching Your Wings to Fly: The Nonspecialist's Guide to Movement Activities for Young Children.* Santa Monica: Goodyear Publishing Co., 1979.

Benton, Michael. "Children's Responses to Stories." *Children's Literature in Education* 10, no. 2 (1979): 68–85.

Bybee, R. W., and R. B. Sund. *Piaget for Educators.* 2d ed. Columbus, OH: Charles Merrill. 1982.

Dimondstein, Geraldine. *Children Dance in the Classroom.* New York: Macmillan, 1971.

Dorian, Margery, and Frances Gulland. *Telling Stories Through Movement.* Belmont, CA: Fearon Publishers, 1974.
  Guided movement to nursery rhymes and short stories, using percussion instruments. From a musical perspective it explores tempo, accents, and rhythmic patterns. Being able to read music is helpful.

Fleming, Gladys Andrews, ed. *Children's Dance.* Washington, DC: American Association for Health, Physical Education and Recreation, Task Force on Children's Dance, 1973.

———. *Creative Rhythmic Movement: Boys and Girls Dancing.* Englewood Cliffs, NJ: Prentice-Hall, 1976.
  A thorough examination of movement techniques one can use to teach children to express and communicate what they feel and think through the medium of dance.

Gardner, Howard. *Frames of Mind: The Theory of Multiple Intelligences.* New York: Basic Books, 1993.
  Has an illuminating chapter on kinesthetic learning called "Body Intelligence."

Haberman, Martin, and Tobie Garth Meisel. *Dance—An Art in Academe.* New York: Teachers College Press, 1970.

Laban, Rudolf von. *The Mastery of Movement.* 3d ed., revised, with an additional chapter by Lisa Ullmann. London: Macdonald & Evans, 1971.

———. *Modern Educational Dance.* London: Macdonald & Evans, 1980.

Landalf, Helen, and Pamela Gerke. *Movement Stories for Young Children Ages 3–6.* Lyme, NH: Smith and Kraus, 1996.
  Teaches movement skills through the medium of stories.

Livo, Norma J., and Sandra A. Rietz. *Storytelling: Process and Practice.* Littleton, CO: Libraries Unlimited, 1986.
  Has an excellent section on singing dances and games.

Marino, Jane. *Babies in the Library!* Lanham, MD: Scarecrow Press, 2003.
  Activity programs for prewalkers and walkers to promote literacy. Programs related to baby's daily activities.

Marino, Jane, and Dorothy F. Houlihan. *Mother Goose Time: Library Programs for Babies and Their Caregivers.* New York: H. W. Wilson, 1992.
  More than 160 rhymes, songs, and finger plays matched to the developmental level of babies.

Marsh, Chester Geppert. *Singing Games and Drills: For Rural Schools, Playground Workers, and Teachers.* New York: A. S. Barnes, 1925.

Murray, Ruth Lowell. *Dance in Elementary Education.* New York: Harper & Row, 1963.

Newlove, Jean, and John Dalby. *Laban for All.* New York: Routledge; London: Nick Hern Books, 2004.
> Laban's theory and practice of movement are introduced to actors. This source is also good for storytellers who wish to convey emotion and the same energy qualities in their actions and movement.

Ross, Ramon Royal. *Storyteller.* Columbus, OH: C. E. Merrill, [1972].
> Contains information on literal dance interpretations and aural images.

Schaefer, Charles E., and Theresa Foy DiGeronimo. *Ages and Stages: A Parent's Guide to Normal Childhood Development.* New York: Wiley, 2000.

Shore, Rima. *Rethinking the Brain: New Insights into Early Development.* New York: Families and Work Institute, 1997

Trotman, Peter. "Loosening Your Grip: Improvising with Language and Movement Language." In *Proximity.* Volume 1: Edition 3. Victoria, Australia: Slightly Moving Productions, 1998. Available at http://proximity.slightly.net/v_one/vol1_ed3.htm.

Index

About the Author

Photo by Teresa Preddy

ARLENE COHEN is a storyteller, librarian, writer, and dancer. She has integrated her skills to offer personal and professional development workshops and performances for 30 years, including presentations for Oregon/Washington library associations and Oregon/Washington educational media associations and in-service trainings for teachers and librarians. She holds a master's degree in children's librarianship from the University of Hawaii, where she taught storytelling in the Speech Department. She has studied and taught ballet, modern dance, creative dance, jazz, hula, t'ai chi, aerobics, and yoga. Her programs have been sponsored by the Hawaii State Foundation on Culture and the Arts, The National Endowment for the Arts, The Hawaiian Zoological Society, and The Regional Arts and Culture Council in Portland, Oregon. She has given workshops and performances in schools, libraries, bookstores, churches, zoos, aquariums, art galleries, festivals, conferences, and museums for all ages. She has been an "Artist-in-the Schools Storyteller" in Hawaii, Arizona, Nevada, and California.